The Northern Tier

One Couple's Bicycle Ride Across America

by
Lief Carlsen

Copyright 2007 by Lief Carlsen

To Mary, of course.

Contents

Northern Tier Route	5
Genesis	6
Exodus	16
Into the Promised Land	26
Crossin' Over Jordan	71
East of Eden	121
Appendices	176
Pioneer	177
Race Across America	183

Northern Tier Route

Genesis

Returning from our cross-country bicycle trip in October 2006, my wife, Mary and I enjoyed a brief period of minor celebrity in our home town of Chelan, Washington. A local paper published several articles detailing our on-the-road exploits and it seemed like everyone knew what we had done and wanted to congratulate us. We were poked, prodded, and pumped for details wherever we went. "What was your favorite place? How many miles did you do each day? Where did the idea to do this come from?" Regarding the latter question, in my case, I'd have to say the idea didn't come from "anywhere." I've always wanted to do something like this and, frankly, I'm more than a little surprised other people don't. My impulse (so far suppressed) when asked that question is to reply "By the way, why haven't *you* ridden a bicycle across America?"

But if you really want to know how we came to do this ride, you'd have to turn to Mary because it was when she decided she wanted to do "The Big Ride" that I knew we would do it. Taking off on a bicycle across America for us was like launching a nuclear ICBM from a Trident submarine, in that the submarine's senior officers wear keys around their necks and *all* of the keys have to be inserted into a special box for the missile to launch. My key to launch this bike ride has always been inserted into the special box. Our departure was just waiting for Mary to insert her key.

For the first nineteen years of our marriage, Mary considered strenuous exercise, especially in the outdoors, as an unpleasant behavior of mine that I would try to get her to join in – comparable, say, to unclogging a toilet or informing the neighbor that you just ran over her cat. She had a discouraging habit of stubbornly resisting my occasional entreaties that we do some fairly vigorous hiking or biking.

That attitude began to change about six years ago, unnoticed by me at first but unmistakable over the course of a year. I've asked her about it and she seems quite certain that it was the emptying of the family nest that spurred her to action. That was the year our youngest son was approaching high school graduation. It was then that Mary realized she was going to have a lot of spare time on her hands when she didn't have children to keep house for anymore. At the suggestion of a friend, she began attending a "spinning" class at a local health club as one way to utilize some of her alarmingly expanding surplus of free time.

In a spinning class you sit on a stationary bicycle with a room full of other sweaty people astride identical machines and pedal (spin) your brains out to the beat of rock and roll music while the class instructor barks commands as to how fast and in what gear you are supposed to spin. Sounds crazy to me but she liked it, liked it so much in fact, that the following summer she bought herself a bicycle that actually moves relative to the surface of the earth and started riding, out of doors, with a local group of bikers called the Apple Capital Bicycle Club.

Over the years I had occasionally dusted off my old 10-speed and ridden several modest rides in the 100 – 200-mile range so I foolishly believed that I retained a residual level of bicycle fitness that would serve me well enough if I ever needed it. After Mary had been riding for several months, I tagged confidently along on a ride one weekend and was horrified to discover that I was being left behind like a dachshund thrown on a racetrack with greyhounds. I was incredulous – Mary, (a girl!) a stronger rider than I? A brief period of panic ensued but by the end of the day I had convinced myself that this turn of events could be explained by the technological superiority of her new bicycle over my old clunker. To prove my point, I immediately went out and bought myself a new bicycle of the same caliber as Mary's and, just in case my point was pure crap, I spent a frantic week secretly building up my strength by riding my new bike up and down the canyon behind our house. On the next group ride, I put in a respectable performance and attempted to distance myself from my shameful performance of the previous week by dismissing suggestions that I was much improved with vague references to having been "under the weather."

Thus began a routine that found us regularly riding along the rivers and through the abundant orchards in north-central Washington in spring, summer, and fall. Mary's transformation from an exercise avoider to an ardent participant is best illustrated by the fact that we rode the very popular Seattle to Portland ride (STP) together that summer. For those who are unfamiliar with this ride, it is a 200-mile event that can be done in one or two days. That year we did it in two. The next year Mary would astound me by doing it in one.

We bought a tandem bicycle in 2004 after encountering a chatty couple on one of our rides who enthusiastically promoted the advantages of two-seaters – faster on flat ground, easier communication between the two riders, and the perfect answer to individuals of different abilities (I had regained my proper role as the stronger rider by then!)

We rode our new tandem on a 360-mile, four-day loop through two very steep passes in the Cascade Mountains on the 4th of July weekend that year and decided, after our very bruised and tender butts had returned to normalcy, that we had what it would take to do something more ambitious. On that same trip, we had encountered a Dutch bicycle tourist at the summit of Washington Pass and were intrigued by his set of extraordinary maps – maps published by the Adventure Cycling Association. They broke the route down to approximately 30-mile sections and showed every conceivable detail that could be of interest to cyclists. My favorite feature was an accompanying graphic profile of a route's elevation changes. On this graph, the route through Washington Pass looked like the Dow Jones Industrial Average of 1929 – repeated over and over again. Having just climbed the east side of the pass, we appreciated what that meant.

Once home, we ordered the organization's catalog and pored over the various offerings. A trans-continental conglomeration of highways and back roads called the Northern Tier Route crossed the country from Anacortes, Washington to Bar Harbor, Maine and passed just north of our home. The seed had been planted. We ordered the set of eleven maps in the Northern Tier Route and set about designing our grand adventure.

As working people, the biggest obstacle to a long trip such as we wanted to do was how to find a sufficiently large block of time to complete the ride and still pay the bills back home. This was actually more of a problem for Mary than me. I am self-employed while Mary works for the State of Washington. I can excuse myself from work anytime I want, the only problem being I don't earn vacation pay. Fortunately, I earn enough when I do work to cover an occasional lengthy vacation. I told Mary I was ready to go "whenever" and that it was up to her to pick a time and schedule time off from her job. We figured we could complete the ride in two months based on the 90-

mile-per-day average we had turned in on our Cascade Loop trip. We decided that mid-August to mid October would be the best weather: in an average year not much precipitation and a little hot at the beginning and perhaps a little colder than one would like at the tail end but probably the best two-month slice of time in the whole year in the northern states.

2005 managed to slip by without presenting the necessary combination of circumstances to do the ride but over that winter Mary one day announced that she had put in a request for a two-month leave of absence from August 18 through October 18, 2006. The die was cast.

All through that winter and spring, our upcoming adventure lurked in my thoughts like a prom date with the prettiest girl in school. I imagined us camping in the Rockies and riding along the Mississippi. I saw us streaking through the autumnal forests of Vermont and watching the waves crash against the rocky shore of Maine. We poured over gear catalogs and debated the merits of various tents or whether a foam or inflatable mattress was more suitable to our needs. We outlined an ambitious training schedule that had us riding successively longer and more frequent rides as the days moved closer to August 18. We made arrangements for the care of our dog and the watering of our lawn. We paid in advance the bills that would come due during our absence.

One thing we didn't do in preparation was read any of the myriad of how-to books written for would-be cyclotourists. Not that I have anything against such reading – it's just something that never occurred to me. My attitude was something like: "get on the bicycle, point it east and start pedaling. How hard can that be?" Mary's attitude was: "The technical stuff is Lief's responsibility." In retrospect, my naiveté, overconfidence or whatever it was, served us well enough – we made it. Not that I couldn't have benefited from a little more expertise on bicycle maintenance for one. In the course of riding any bicycle 4000 miles, it's going to need some adjustment and on several occasions I spent some head-scratching hours along the side of back roads teaching myself by trial and error how all those little cables and screws affect bicycle performance.

We also told everyone in our lives what we planned to do and a surprising number of them asked if we could keep them informed via email of our day-to-day progress. Our friends' interest and the fact that I have always harbored a secret desire to write for an audience led me to approach our local newspaper, the Wenatchee World, with an offer to send them regular dispatches from the road. Sports editor Steve Maher liked the idea immediately and sent a reporter and photographer out to do a story about us just prior to our departure. It was while Mary and I were talking with Steve that Mary brought to Steve's (and my) attention that we would be arriving at our final destination in Bar Harbor on or about our 25th wedding anniversary – October 10. This had not occurred to me before that moment but sounded like a nice touch to what already promised to be a day of some significance.

With my journal entries now guaranteed an audience, I added a very significant five pounds of laptop computer to our growing load of gear. The importance that writing my dispatches had for me is evidenced by the fact that the computer was by far the single, heaviest item we would carry.

In the final weeks before our departure Mary had a very busy schedule trying to tie up any lose ends at work so that things would run smoothly during her absence. I was working a frenzied schedule trying to sock away some serious money. To a surprising extent, we were both successful in our respective endeavors. The unfortunate consequence of that success, however, was the shelving of our ambitious training schedule. We had expected we would be riding four or five days a week and doing several weekend mini-trips of several hundred miles in the last weeks. What we ended up doing was taking a single 45-mile ride one day a week during the last month. Abandoning our training schedule reminded me of my student days when each Friday I would leave school determined to spend the weekend studying only to find my assignments untouched come Monday morning. We consoled ourselves with the idea that we would start off easy during the first few days of our ride and fall back on that time-tested method used by the U.S. Army: OJT, on-the-job-training.

We also killed several other troublesome "birds" with a single, minor route change. Adventure Cycling's Northern Tier Route begins on Puget Sound at Anacortes, Washington. For us to start from there we would have to deal with the significant logistical problem of how to transport ourselves and our oversized bicycle the 250 miles from our home to Anacortes. Besides, we had already ridden that distance on several occasions in the past. Our solution was to start our adventure from our doorstep in Chelan. The bonus was that we would avoid, out of the gate, the unappealing climb over five serious mountain passes that are prescribed by the orthodox route. Our plan would be to leave Chelan and follow US 2 to Spokane, then turn north where we would rendezvous with the Northern Tier at Newport on the Washington-Idaho border.

Finally, no discussion of this trip's germination would be complete without mentioning several profoundly disquieting and relevant accidents that occurred in the year leading up to our departure. I suppose it is common sense that riding a bicycle, an intentionally light-weight machine on top of which the rider perches himself with no more inherent stability than a pigeon on a power line, is a means of locomotion fraught with risk. After all, we don't wear helmets when we ride in cars, boats or airplanes. And what kid hasn't skinned his knee or bruised his elbow riding his bike around the neighborhood? Still, it came as a shock to the members of our cycling community when one of our own, an ultra-experienced and sensible rider, collided while riding within a mile of his house with a car turning into a driveway. He was paralyzed from the neck down as a result of the collision and lingered in a hospital bed for weeks in this God-awful state before finally (some, I among them, would say mercifully) succumbing to an infection. Two women we didn't know, in separate incidents, were struck and killed while riding on highway shoulders by inattentive drivers within twenty miles of our home. We heard of numerous other bicycle deaths during that year in news reports from all around the country. Perhaps we were hyper-sensitive because of our upcoming trip but it seemed like bicycles were, with alarming frequency, becoming fair game for automobiles.

Mary adopted a fatalistic response to these events. "I could die today in any number of accidents" she would say whenever we heard of one of these unfortunate deaths. "I'm not going to stop living to keep from dying."

I was equally undeterred by the prospect of an accident. My way of dealing with the risk was to try to put it in proper perspective and take a few prudent precautions. First of all, it is important to remember that bicycle deaths receive considerable attention because they are unusual. I'm no authority on the relative risk of various everyday activities but I doubt that riding a bicycle throughout life is as risky as smoking cigarettes.

One of the big dangers for riders of two-wheeled vehicles is that automobile drivers are expecting the road to be populated by other *automobiles*. They aren't looking for motorcycles and bicycles and what you're not looking for you often overlook. I notice this about myself when my wife sends me to the refrigerator to look for something like a bottle of ketchup. If I'm expecting it to be in a container of a certain size, shape and color I will often fail to see it even though it is in plain view if any of those identifiers is altered. I am convinced this quirk of the human brain is involved in many car-bicycle collisions.

So, the solution to this type of threat would be to make one's self impossible *not* to notice. The best thing we could find toward this end is the orange, reflective vests worn by highway construction workers. Mary and I actually already owned two of these. I had bought them years earlier after hearing about an accident but Mary had declined to wear hers after a few outings because she considered it "unfashionable." The death of our friend convinced her to cast fashion to the wind in exchange for survivability, at least while she was on the bicycle, and we faithfully donned our orange, net, construction vests every time we mounted our bicycles until the last day of the trip when she inadvertently left hers in our hotel room and didn't notice until we were several miles down the road.

The second vital component of our Automobile Avoidance Program, as I dubbed it, was a pennant attached to a wavy fiberglass pole attached to the little gear trailer we planned to tow. The fact that this would wave back and forth added a second line of defense to our noticeability. I also liked the way it leaned outward, several feet into the traffic, discouraging any smart alecks who might think it great fun to see how close they could pass without hitting us. I even considered if there were a practicable way to attach a steel ball bearing to the top of the flagpole for the purpose of inflicting damage to would-be smart alecks. Regrettably, I never figured out how to do that.

Thus, the summer of 2006 matured into its final trimester with us eagerly anticipating our coming road trip. Our friend's death had reminded us that cycling is not without risk but we also realized that any life worth living involves an element of risk. We were convinced this was a risk worth taking.

Exodus
8/18/06, Chelan to Coulee City

We rolled out of bed a bit earlier than usual on Friday morning, August 18, 2006 – three hours earlier, to be precise. I had already been awake for some time when, at 4:00 A.M., I asked Mary if she were sleeping. She wasn't, and we decided there was no point denying the obvious: we were excited as a couple of kids on Christmas morning and sleep would not be forthcoming.

Besides, we still had packing to do. Despite countless hours of rumination on the subject of what to bring on our grand adventure, we had never actually pre-arranged all of the items we intended to use. Oh, I had stuffed the major items like the tent, sleeping bags and air mattresses into their waterproof bag in our little one-wheeled trailer, but we had never actually put the finishing touches like toothbrushes and flashlight batteries together in their proper containers. My preliminary packing had convinced us that we would have no trouble fitting everything we needed, and perhaps a little more, into our panniers (saddlebags) and trailer. Now, as I watched Mary valiantly trying to stuff one more item into her pannier (which she straddled like a French farmer trying to force-feed an uncooperative goose), I could see that we had underestimated the extent of our "necessities." Or, to be more precise, I had forgotten that Mary is a woman, the type of person who brings five bathing suits on our Mexican vacation each winter. A few harsh words were exchanged, the essences of which were that Mary had too much stuff or, from her perspective, that I needed to "butt out."

To her credit, Mary did manage to squeeze all her stuff into her pannier and by 8:30 (a full four and a half hours after rising) we had assembled our little caravan to the point where we were able to start moving.

The first quarter mile of our 4000-mile ride was, in fact, a walk. The dirt road connecting our house in the hills above Lake Chelan with the county road leading to town has enough sandy soft spots to make it as treacherous as a quagmire for a skinny-tired bicycle like our tandem. Mary, ever the cautious one, insisted on walking and even I realized that a crash at the very outset of our ride would be bad for morale, so we walked, side by side, pushing our outsized bicycle and trailer to the gate of our land.

By the time we got to the county road it was abundantly clear to me that our little trailer full of camping gear had somehow gained considerable weight during its final packing. Pushing the bike up hill felt like push starting my old Volkswagen on a cold morning and the whole combination of bike and trailer had to be held perfectly upright or it immediately became hopelessly unbalanced and could only be righted through supreme effort. I knew that I hadn't added anything of significance to its contents. That left Mary, in whose direction I now turned with eyelids half-lowered in a look of accusation. She raised both hands in a show of innocence and swore she had packed only necessities, whereupon I threatened to disembowel the trailer of its contents in my own crude way if she didn't come up with several pounds of superfluous items. She responded with a few choice accusations of her own and there we stood, two people dressed in brightly colored Spandex on a dirt road with an oversized bicycle trading angry words and going nowhere. It occurred to both of us that this was not a good way to start a ride across America.

The answer to our little impasse turned out to be putting Mary at the helm of the bicycle for a few paces and letting her feel its unwieldiness. A few seconds of trying to push forward and balance the ungainly bicycle had the desired effect. She turned to me and agreed that the bike was entirely too heavy. Something had to go and this, as it turned out, was a hefty supply of energy bars and several clothing item she had added at the last moment. This shedding of weight amounted to a nominal reduction in our overall ballast but it was significant for its psychological impact – we were at last serious about doing our best, getting the most out of our bodies and equipment.

Standing as we were at the cusp of our departure, any delay at that moment seemed intolerable. But we couldn't leave her clothes and the energy bars at the side of the road like so much litter, so, as soon as Mary bagged up the offending items, I grabbed them and ran back to the house, then returned back to Mary, only to arrive so out of breath I could barely stand upright.

As soon as I caught my breath we hopped on the bike and started our six-mile descent to the town of Chelan, during which, as if by magic, the rancor of our previous exchange was suddenly forgotten and transformed into euphoria as we sped through the cool morning air. What we had dreamed of for so long was now happening. We were finally on our way. I wanted to sing, shout and dance for joy. I believe I did sing a little.

Stopping at the Post Office to mail a few things we noticed the first casualty of our ride: our orange safety pennant on the trailer was gone. It had apparently been blown off its fiberglass pole during our descent. The flag was the centerpiece of our Automobile Avoidance Program so this was no trifling matter. Retracing our route up the steep road to retrieve the flag, on the other hand, was out of the question. We told ourselves we'd have to find some other brightly colored object along the way to take its place.

With the last of our pre-departure chores taken care of, we mounted our bike and left the world of responsibilities and obligations behind to head into a different realm where freedom and the challenge of the unknown would be our daily fare. I was trembling with anticipation. We pushed away from the curb and into the traffic flow leading out of town. So slowly and smoothly did our large bicycle respond to our efforts at that moment that it could best be compared to an ocean liner being maneuvered into the harbor by tug boats. I shifted to a low gear and we gradually built up speed.

Lake Chelan, a magnificent fjord of a lake that snakes 55 miles from the arid plateau of eastern Washington into the heart of the North Cascades, has a most peculiar appearance when viewed from across the Columbia River at the top of McNeil Canyon. It appears to be bottled up and ready to spill like a jug of milk into the depths of the Columbia Gorge, which it would were it not held back by a natural dam of granite that is the Chelan Butte. Glaciers carved the trench that the lake now occupies to a depth of 1500 feet (the bottom of which is 400 feet below sea level!) A mere two miles from the lake, the Columbia River, through old fashioned river erosion, wore away its stream bed so that it now runs 350 feet lower than the lake's surface. It was through the precipitous drop from the lake to the river that we plunged as we left our home town and headed into the great unknown.

Down, down, down we accelerated toward the Beebe Bridge which crosses the Columbia. I had to apply all three of our brakes to keep our elongated bicycle's speed under forty M.P.H. because, while it may be slow on an incline, our bike is a veritable runaway freight train on a decline. This is because with two riders and a trailer in tow it has about the same frontal area to catch the wind (and slow it down) as a single bike and rider but roughly two and one half times the mass for gravity to pull on.

The decline ended and the incline came on soon enough with the crossing of the Beebe Bridge. The thrill of our drop into the gorge was replaced by the daunting slope of McNeil Canyon which would take us, on grades as steep as twelve percent, back up to approximately the same elevation as we had started from in Union Valley. In other words, in the first ten miles of our trip, we dropped and climbed a combined total of 5500 feet. As far as I know, there is no stretch of similar length on our entire projected route across the United States that will surpass those numbers.

We charged the canyon's slopes with everything we had but within the first few miles we were faced with sections of the road that, even in the bike's lowest gear, we simply could not pedal up. In our lowest gear, at a reasonable cadence, our bike moves at about 4 MPH. Well, we couldn't keep up a reasonable cadence and so dropped into a range where walking is just as fast as pedaling – and easier. So there we were, a scant six or seven miles into our journey, walking our bicycle for the second time and *laughing* about it. It was hot, our leg muscles were throbbing, and our chests were heaving but, no matter, we were delirious with joy to be on our way. Anyone who knows Mary would have known that we were in a most unusual state of mind because Mary balked not at all when I hitched her to the front of the bike with a bungee cord. We ponderously plodded our way up the canyon for over an hour in that way – with Mary harnessed like some beast of burden and I pushing from the handlebars.

When we at last cleared the top of the canyon, we paused briefly to enjoy that peculiar view of Lake Chelan that I wrote of earlier and then pedaled out onto the Columbia Plateau toward the first town of the first day: Mansfield.

We were barely twenty miles from home and still in familiar territory when we pulled up to the little grocery store in Mansfield. Mansfield is wheat country as opposed to Chelan which is apple/tourist country. Like communities everywhere that derive their income primarily from agriculture, Mansfield is a shrunken remnant of its former self. The few retail businesses that remain on its truncated main street appear to be hanging on by their fingernails. I take no joy in these towns' struggling economies, in fact they strike a chord of sadness in me, but I like net result. I like the quiet, peaceful, friendly vibes that hang in the air about their antiquated store fronts. I like the slow pace of life they exude from every squeaky floorboard sanded smooth over many years by the dusty boots of shuffling farmers.

We bought ourselves some bottles of Gatorade, cans of V8, Chef Boyardee Mini Ravioli, and bananas then repaired to the shaded bench in front of the store to watch a brief episode of small-town life. Shortly, from opposite ends of town, like gunslingers in an old western, two aimless pairs of young boys walking bicycles slowly meandered their way toward each other. There was no gunfire, of course, just a languid exchange of words when they met. One boy displayed a toy car to the others then they went their separate ways. Mansfield may not be the best place to own a business but I bet it's not a bad place to be a boy with a bicycle on a summer afternoon.

Our destination for the day, Coulee City, is forty miles from Mansfield. We figured that with our bellies freshly full of lunch and two water bottles each, we were in good shape to go the distance. What we didn't figure on was the effect of a hot, dry wind blowing in our faces. Just over half way to Coulee City I had already drained my two bottles and was eyeing the remaining contents of Mary's second bottle when we came upon a group of farmers mixing a tub of bizarrely red liquid. They were using water mixed with a powder to make their peculiar brew and I left the bike in Mary's hands to wander (stagger?) over and talk to them with the clear intention of getting some of their precious water. I was so thirsty I probably would have slugged down half a gallon of their red brew had they not warned me it was an insecticide. "What about some of that?" I asked, indicating the marvelously clear water coming from a red rubber hose. The big guy mixing the powder in the tub said he could go one better if I could wait a minute until he was done at which time he'd get me some fresh, cold water out of his well. With admirable patience I joined in their playful banter for a few thirst-crazed minutes while the red powder ever-so-slowly dissolved in the tub. Then the big guy took me out back to a tap that rose out of the ground and pulled back the lever that released a torrent of beautiful, clear, water.

"Hold on a minute" he said as I lunged to fill my bottles. "You want to wait for the cold stuff."

"Oh yeah, sure" I said, as nonchalantly as I could manage, as if I did not have a near irresistible urge to wrap my lips around the tap and make of myself a water-filled balloon.

And sweet water it was. I can't ever remember water tasting quite as good as that well water. As I walked past the farmers at the tank, I thanked them for their water and they wished me luck in a way that made me think that they thought I would need it. One of them called after me,

"Say, ain't you the folks that I read about in the paper who's goin' to Maine?" We were indeed, I answered. I was pleased to know our fame had preceded us and impressed by the power of the printed word.

Back on the road again I had a new problem. My left foot was going numb. The shoes I was wearing were a pair of running shoes Mary had bought for me a year earlier. I hadn't worn them during the intervening months because I hadn't been running and had no other use for them. But they had seemed the perfect footwear for this trip inasmuch as they were all-purpose shoes that I could wear while riding or after hours in a stroll through town. The flaw in my brilliant plan was that the size 11 shoes (my usual size) were actually size 10 shoes and prevented any useful quantity of blood from reaching my feet. We stopped a short distance up the road and I switched my running shoes for a pair of shower zorries I had brought along to keep my feet raised above the fungus-saturated surfaces of the public shower facilities we expected to use during the next two months.

The zorries were quite effective at allowing blood to flow freely to my feet and had the added benefit of not blocking the passage of air between my toes which was a pleasantly sensual experience I had never felt before. They had the serious drawback, however, of drooping over the front of my pedals and catching on the pavement from time to time, occasionally pulling my feet with them and skinning the fronts of my toes. At the rate I was losing flesh, I figured I would have no toes left by the time I got to Coulee City. Of course, that probably would have enabled my size 11 feet to fit comfortably into my size 10 shoes but it didn't seem like a fair trade. I stopped again to ponder my predicament.

"Put your shoes on without your socks" Mary said. Her tone suggested something closer to "Put your shoes on without your socks, moron."

"You can't wear shoes without socks!" I protested.

"Why not?" she shot back.

I could think of no good reason except that I had always worn socks in my shoes. I tried the arrangement she had suggested and found that it actually felt rather nice. The blood flow to my feet was greatly improved and my feet felt considerably cooler. I stood at the side of the road appreciatively wiggling my naked toes inside my shoes with all the fascination of a two-year-old watching his fart bubbles rise to the surface of his bath water. All that was left to be done was to shrug my shoulders and say "OK. Feels good. Let's go."

With my feet once again sentient and our bodies adequately hydrated we completed the remaining distance to Coulee City without further incident. We checked into the comfortably grassy campground at the foot of Banks Lake, showered, set up the tent, ate a bite of food and fell soundly asleep – all before the sun had even set. Our first day had been a mere 60-miler and fraught with miscalculation but a thunderous success all the same.

Mary at the end of day one – tired but happy.

Into the Promised Land
Washington, Idaho, Montana

August 19, 2006; Day 2; Mile 151; Coulee City to Spokane: Banks Lake is not your average lake. At twenty-five miles in length and with an average width of several miles, it is no backyard pond. But size is not its principal distinction; Banks Lake is notable because of how it gets its water and how it contains it.

The Columbia River has been around for many millions of years and, for a time, glaciers blocked its flow through its traditional bed. During those years it struck out cross-country beginning at what is now the location of the Grand Coulee Dam. Once the glaciers receded, the river reverted to its original, preferred course and left behind an elongated gash in the basalt surface of the Columbia Plateau known as Grand Coulee.

With the building of giant Grand Coulee Dam in the 1930's, unimaginable quantities of cheap hydroelectric power became available and engineers used some of it to pump vast quantities of Columbia River water hundreds of feet up cliffs along the river in gargantuan pipes to the river's abandoned bed in Grand Coulee across which they had built a low, earthen dam at the present site of Coulee City. This is the very Coulee City where Mary and I camped last night. The lake formed by the pumped water, Banks Lake, is used to irrigate millions of acres of fertile crop land in an area known as the Columbia Basin near present-day Quincy.

We left Coulee City feeling surprisingly good for two middle-aged people who, with minimal training, had just completed an arduous 61 miles on their first day. From Coulee City, US 2 starts a gentle but considerable rise of nearly a thousand feet to Creston after which the elevation stays pretty much constant at about 2500 feet all the way to Airway Heights on the outskirts of Spokane. It is an area we had driven through many times and one that fascinates me. Treeless, windswept, devoid of rivers, it is nonetheless a perfect place to grow wheat – a Garden of Wheaten. Wheat farmers on this plateau consistently harvest considerably more bushels per acre than wheat farmers in most parts of the world.

It is also a nearly car-less highway and thus a fine bicycle road since Interstate 90 at forty miles to the south carries most of the cross-state traffic. The little towns that service the area's farmers are spaced about ten to fifteen miles apart along US 2 which must have been the maximum distance farmers of old were willing to travel on a regular basis in their horse-drawn conveyances to get supplies. In a happy coincidence not unnoticed by Mary and me, that is also about the right distance between rest stops for two bicycle riders on their second day on the road. Scarcely had we left one town than the distant outline of tall trees and grain elevators of the next town would appear on the horizon. Wasn't that the way Oz appeared to Dorothy and her friends as they made their way along the yellow brick road? And Dorothy was from Kansas where they grow a lot of wheat too, right?

We were thankful for each little town as we moved through this Oz-like land because stopping at their shaded and grassy parks to eat and drink broke the long, hot day into manageable chunks. There are few things as enjoyable as drinking a carton of cold chocolate milk on a hot afternoon under a big maple tree in Wilbur's City Park.

Harleybeetle

There was a guy in the parking lot of the market in Wilbur who was traveling around the country in a peculiar vehicle he had cobbled together from spare parts. It could best be described as a VW beetle in the process of ingesting a Harley-Davidson motorcycle. The entire machine was painted in red, white and blue stripes and he drove it from the motorcycle part out in front while he used the VW part in rear as his sleeping quarters. In addition to a bed he had a large, flat-screen TV in there, which, he explained was a necessity because "It gets lonely sometimes on the road." He was proud of his heterodox amalgamation and appeared to think of it as something worthy of historical note. To this end, he had a hefty scrapbook full of photos of his noteworthy encounters and a poster explaining the extent of his travels. A kindred spirit? This is a big and varied country we live in. There is something inspirational about the idea of crossing it up-close and personal that attracts a certain sort of person. This guy obviously thinks there is something for the soul to be found on the highways of America. I hope he finds it. Perhaps he has. What about us?

Who knows where tomorrow's great leaders will come from – Reardon, perhaps? We stopped there for our last heat break of the day and came upon some kids playing basketball in the park. There was one little guy in the game who struck me as truly extraordinary. First of all, there was his appearance. He obviously did not have the ideal physique for a basketball player. He was stocky in the extreme and much shorter than his playmates. He wore a pair of sunglasses while playing ball like some sawed-off Secret Service agent trying to blend in with the population of this small, agricultural town. But it was his personality that really stood out. He had an aura that said "Take me seriously." One would expect a kid of his stature playing with much bigger kids to be a marginal participant but he always seemed to be in the thick of the game. Something about him demanded attention. It wasn't his skill because, even though he took a lot of shots, most of them missed the basket by wide margins. The first time I saw him shoot and completely miss the backboard I expected jeers from the others. It never happened. Instead, he charged through everybody to retrieve the ball and came back to take another shot – which he missed. He was unstoppable. I wouldn't be surprised to see his picture on the cover of Time magazine some day.

It is ninety miles from Coulee City to Airway Heights and Mary was complaining of severe saddle soreness by the time we'd gone the sixty miles to Davenport but I wasn't worried. I knew we'd make it because we had promised ourselves we would spend the night in the Hilton if we made it there today and comfort and luxury are powerful attractants to Mary. Toward that end, we paused in Davenport for about an hour to have one of those all-American meals of nourishment: the cheeseburger-and-fries-with-milkshake combo meal. It did the job – we arrived in Airway Heights with daylight to spare. Within minutes of our arrival, I could hear Mary exhaling a long "ahhhhhh" as she lowered her long-suffering butt into a bathtub full of hot water.

August 20, 2006; Day 3; Spokane, WA to Spirit Lake, Idaho: At breakfast this morning in the sunny dining room of the Hilton (yes, *Hilton,* as in hotel) the waitress noticed our clingy, colorful bicycle attire and asked the "where from?" and "where to?" questions. This was all Mary needed to launch into a lively account of our planned journey. She obviously very much enjoyed telling the waitress all about it. I'm a little uncomfortable with this approach. I guess I think we haven't earned the right to talk about ourselves as cross-country riders yet. It seems a little on the presumptuous side to me since we've only completed 150 miles so far and we have about 4000 to go.

We are fortunate it was a Sunday morning when we rode through Spokane. Only the hard-core church goers were up and about. Once we arrived at the city's center we got on the bicycle trail that takes you all the way to Coeur d'Alene. The trail weaves through the old Spokane World's Fair site, past the campus of Gonzaga University, and along the Spokane River. It's a model for bicycle trails everywhere. Actually, we hadn't gone but half a mile on the trail when we were wrenched to a stop by one of the straps of our panniers snagging a spoke of the bike's rear wheel. It stopped the wheel cold and we skidded to a stop, wearing all the rubber off the bottom of the tire right down to the cords. Thus Mary, who had insisted we carry a spare tire, was proved right (I had argued tires wear out slowly, not all at once.) Since we had to put our spare on the wheel, now we're looking for a store that carries a 700 X 30 tire to replace that one.

The day soon turned quite hot. By the time we got to Post Falls we were pretty well dehydrated. We lingered a little longer than necessary in one of those supermarket-drugstore-variety store places just to enjoy the air conditioning. In addition to lunch and liquids, I bought a bag of colored balloons, several of which I inflated and tied to our fiberglass pole which so recently carried our little orange safety pennant. Any driver whose car runs us over is not going to have the excuse that he didn't see us.

One way to temporarily beat the heat is to soak your shirt in water and then put it on. We've done this several times today. WARNING! Do not do this if the day is not *very* hot. The shock is enough to stop a healthy heart even on a hot day like today but it is extremely effective. The only problem is that the shirt dries out in about twenty minutes and more water is needed. I find it nothing short of amazing how effective evaporating water is at cooling. Do you know that the American military actually *froze* water on the oppressively-hot islands of the South Pacific during WWII using evaporative cooling towers? Well, I guess that's a story for another day. Anyway, a less extreme technique is to ride with only our netted, orange safety vests on (lest the reader think my wife rides bare-breasted I should mention here that Mary wears a sports bra at times such as this).

We made it about ten miles north of Post Falls to Rathdrum and pulled off onto a shady patch of lawn behind a fast food place where we killed a couple of the afternoon's hottest hours. A guy with a lawn mower cut the grass all around us until, finally, the only piece left was the shady area we were spread out over so we packed up and hit the road – SR 41, soon to be christened by us the Highway to Hell. The lady in the information station at the state line had assured us that SR 41 had light traffic. The traffic was heavy as we left town but we assumed it would thin out after a few miles. Well, imagine the traffic on a typical freeway and squeeze it onto a narrow, two-lane highway with a six to twelve-inch shoulder and you have SR 41 on a Sunday afternoon. Never mind bicyclists, what does a motorist do if he has car trouble on that highway? Drive over the embankment? Block the highway? We spent the afternoon pedaling along (clinging to?) our six-inch strip of highway while a steady stream of 60-mph cars zoomed by, some literally within a foot of us. Several times we dismounted and pushed our bike on our six-inch allotment of pavement while we walked on the dirt to reduce our chances of losing an arm to a passing car. On top of it all, it was hot and we were tired. I'd have to say it was a somewhat discouraging afternoon. Having ridden bicycles on a regular basis on the public highways, we thought we were prepared for times like this with our orange safety vests but, now that it's over, I realize I am exhausted and Mary's confidence is clearly rattled.

When we set our sights on reaching Spirit Lake at day's end I had imagined it to be a town on the shore of a scenic lake steeped in Indian legends about the supernatural. I imagined it to be just the kind of place to pitch your tent and enjoy a view that conjured visions of Indians of a bygone era in their war canoes crossing the lake. Well, in the first place, Spirit *Lake* is not visible from the Town of

Spirit Lake. Townsfolk told us the lake is a rather ugly lake and not worth the trouble to go see, which, I should add, is true of the town as well. To its credit, the town does have a large park which we are unofficially camped in. Unofficially, because no one gave us permission to camp here but there are no campgrounds near town so we don't know where else to stay. We are just hanging out waiting for the cover of darkness at which time we plan to unfurl our tent in the park's gazebo and hope no one kicks us out. Our unorthodox choice of tent site is to avoid harassment by prowling police cars and/or getting showered by the park's sprinklers should they come on in the night.

While I was talking to a guy on the other side of the park about other possible campgrounds near town I happened to look over at Mary sitting on the steps of the gazebo with a forlorn look on her face. I gotta' tell ya, she has me concerned. My concern is that she will overreact to the hardship of today's heat and traffic and lack of a proper campground and get discouraged. She has a knack for seeing the worst in a situation. I did my best before we set out on this trip to warn her that there would be some tough times and she reassured me that she was well aware of that. But I worry that she'll crap out on me. It has happened. Twice when we were hiking different segments of the Pacific Crest Trail she would have quit if that had been an option. Only the fact that she had no alternative but to press on kept her moving. What will happen if we hit a long stretch of bad weather or mechanical trouble or illness?

I walked down to the town's convenience store and grabbed some sweet rolls for tomorrow's breakfast and rented the DVD *Wallace & Grommit: The Curse of the Were-rabbit*. We're watching it on my laptop more or less just to prove that people who stay in motels are no better than we are with their HBO and Pay-For-View movies. We may be just a couple of bicycle riders in a tent who take spit baths in the park's Porta Potty but we can watch movies too!

August 21, 2006; Day 4; Spirit Lake to Hope, Idaho:
The proper place to begin today's entry is with a postscript to yesterday's entry where I made mention of our plan to avoid the park's sprinklers by pitching out tent in the park's gazebo. Well, we were too clever by half it seems: the park did have sprinklers which came on in the wee hours with the force of water cannons showing no mercy. They hit our tent from several directions at once and went on for what seemed like an hour. At least we know our tent is waterproof.

After the debilitating heat of yesterday, we were surprised to awaken to a numbing cold this morning in Spirit Lake. We dressed in all our clothes and for once, actually looked forward to pedaling uphill as it would generate some body heat. Wouldn't you know it, there were no hills. My fingers suffered the most from the cold and I vowed to buy a pair of warm gloves at the first opportunity.

We ducked into a roadside café after about five miles, not because we were especially hungry but because the thought of a hot meal and hot drinks sounded particularly inviting. There were about fifteen old guys already seated in the café when we arrived. They obviously all knew each other and were on good terms as quips and gossip were flying freely between the various tables. We got the impression they were a local institution of sorts who spent their mornings at that café regularly enough that the waitress knew ahead of time what each wanted.

The hot victuals helped get our motors running as did the rising sun. Properly nourished and limbered up, we got back on our bike and headed toward Newport – a town of some significance to us. Newport is where we join the Northern Tier Route of the Adventure Cycling Association – an organization that produced a map set that we purchased for our ride. They have wonderfully detailed maps which break the 4200 miles from Anacortes, Washington to Bar Harbor, Maine into thirty-mile sections. They include explicit, turn-by-turn written instructions as well as where all pertinent services are to be found. Another great feature of the route they outline: wherever possible, they avoid traffic-congested roads. After the Highway to Hell leading into Spirit Lake, we were very appreciative of that feature. It took us a few head-scratching attempts to learn to read the maps but by the end of the day we were mining them for all sorts of useful information.

Our introduction to the Northern Tier Route was the Old Priest River Road which is a serene expanse of asphalt which inexplicably follows the Pend Oreille River. Whatever, we immediately appreciated having the road to ourselves. It was quiet and scenic, cool and sunny – just what we needed to restore our faith in the institution of bicycling.

Along about noon the temperature had climbed back up into the hot zone when we broke out of the deep Idaho forest and onto a causeway that crosses Lake Pend Oreille to the resort city of Sandpoint. The lake breeze was refreshing (does it sound like I was preoccupied with temperature?) and we arrived in Sandpoint feeling pretty good with the possible exception of my left thigh that was starting to ache. Sandpoint is a lively little city with a busy, old fashioned shopping district. We visited a bicycle store and replaced our spare rear tire that we had to use after the incident in Spokane's Riverfront Park. We bought a spare tire for the front wheel as well.

We took a little break from pedaling to walk through the town and check out the diverse selection of people and colorful window displays. It felt good to walk for a change.

At the far end of Sandpoint an old guy came up to me in a supermarket and started speaking German, no doubt in response to my jersey which sports the yellow, red and black of the Federal Republic's flag as well as the word "Germany" across the front. I gamely attempted to respond to him in my halting German but immediately gave away my true nationality. Nevertheless, he seemed appreciative that I obviously didn't have an anti-German bias. I guess the old guy had had a hard time in this country because of his German roots which surprised me because I've never heard much anti-German talk. As a matter of fact, wasn't there something about the Aryan Brotherhood in Idaho a few years back? One would think an old Nazi would feel right at home here. He confided to me that he'd served in the Wehrmacht in WWII and was a little vague about whether he had actually been a member of the Nazi party but he very much appreciated me wearing his birth country's colors. He wished us well on our journey.

Mary demonstrates she's not too good to share a lake with dogs.

Leaving Sandpoint proved to be problematic because, just as we figured out how to read our maps, we encountered a large detour where a considerable chunk of the city's roads were being torn up and replaced. We rolled up to the head of the line to see if we might slip by the detour seeing as how we are on a skinny bicycle and could actually transform ourselves into pedestrians if need be. The flagger responded to this inquiry as if I had suggested she perform a lewd act in public. Chastised, I saw little point in explaining to her that, being strangers who were slavishly following a guide map, we would be hopelessly lost if we set off on an unfamiliar detour through the city. Luckily, a woman in a mini van understood our plight and gave us remarkably simple and easy-to-follow instructions for how to get to back on route. Thank God for people like her. (May the flagger burn in hell!)

About ten miles out of Sandpoint the heat was getting to us again when we saw a car suddenly swerve off the highway and down a short dirt road to the lake. The car came to a sudden stop in a cloud of dust at the water's edge and a rotund young couple hopped out and released their dogs that went straight into the lake for a swim. Obviously, they'd done this before. Taking my lead from the dogs, I parked the bike and jumped in. Mary, who would normally shudder at the suggestion she share a lake with dogs, soon followed. I am happy to report that dogs and humans derived much pleasure from that refreshing water.

A few miles up the road we found a tidy and blessedly shady lakeside campground with a little store and showers for $10. As the sun was going down we strolled out on a grass-covered breakwater that protected the resort's little boat harbor and sat on a park bench to catch up on our people watching skills. It was a serene ending to a satisfying day.

August 22, 2006; Day 5; Hope, Idaho to Troy, Montana: We crossed the border into Montana today and even though there was no sign to announce it, we could *feel* it. Montana is just better looking than Idaho. This state looks like the Old West. The valleys aren't hemmed in by crowding trees the way they are in Idaho. They have *just the right amount* of trees separating expansive pastures which are home to massive buffalo and sleek horses whose manes and tails stream out behind them as they run. The barns are cowboy barns with steep, shingled roofs and sunlight streaming through their weathered, gray siding. I like Montana! I knew I would.

After crossing the river at Clark Fork early this morning we got onto a quiet little road with almost no traffic. We crossed Cabinet Gorge on a high bridge where two young guys with harnesses were sitting. I thought they were base jumpers (those daredevils who jump off high places) so I stopped to talk to them. They were actually structural engineers who contracted with the Montana Highway Department to evaluate the bridge's integrity. They strap themselves to the underside of the bridge and swing around like monkeys while looking for damage. They looked like they were having a great time and probably making good money in the process. Not a bad way to make a living I would say. It would probably take me a while to get used to hanging by a strap from the bottom of a high bridge but I think I could dig the life – beautiful country, technical expertise, working out-of-doors. It's a shame it takes a lifetime to learn what it is you like in this world. A common dilemma for college freshmen is that they have no idea what they want to do. I can think of any number of majors I would like to pursue if I were a young man again: field geologist, linguist, petroleum engineer, military officer, entrepreneur, jet pilot, journalist, etc.

Mary beats the heat in Bull Lake, Montana

We pulled off the highway at Bull Lake and took another swim in the heat of the afternoon. Nice, clear water. It reminded me of our own, beautiful Lake Chelan in Washington.

We were too tired to press on the eleven miles to Libby at day's end so we chose to go two miles off route into the town of Troy for camping. Had we known beforehand that Troy lies at the bottom of a long and steep hill that we would have to pedal back up in the morning we might have summoned the needed energy to continue ahead to Libby. As it was, we didn't catch on to that bit of geographical trivia until we were well down the hill and the damage, as it were, already done. We stopped at Troy's tourism office to get some information about campgrounds and came away with little useful information and the impression that Troy is a town looking for an economic miracle. Apparently, mining and logging built the town but both of those are in decline and so they're betting on tourism to pick up the slack. I'd say they have a way to go. The whole town looks pretty run down. We looked around and about the only place we could find was a campground with a pathetic, faded, little sign that looked like it really didn't want anyone to stop there.

Well, don't judge a campground by its sign. The pleasant little old lady who ran the place charged us all of eight dollars to camp. The way she carefully filled out our registration form and receipt you would have thought we were buying the place. For our eight dollars we got a tent site on a lush patch of clover, a spotless shower room, and a laundromat. We were very pleased with the transaction. I didn't want to tell her how to run her business but I think her tidy little campground warranted a bigger, brighter sign.

Our campsite was next to a twenty foot travel trailer that appeared to be the permanent residence of a disheveled couple who mistakenly thought their thin trailer walls were soundproof. As I was pitching the tent and Mary was off investigating the shower facility I heard them yelling at each other about whose responsibility it was to shut the door on their storage shed (which made me wonder if all the commotion was a response to us moving in next to them, implying that we might help ourselves to some of the junk they had stored in their miserable little shed.) A few minutes later the woman stalked out and slammed the shed door. Her man soon followed with an unsteady gait. He looked like he'd started drinking early and hard that day. He walked over to me and asked me if I'd like to share a joint with them. I thanked him but declined. My refusal seemed to confound him and he was at a loss for something to say. I could only surmise that no one in Troy had ever turned down his offer of a joint before. We stood under the little tree in front of his trailer awkwardly facing each other. What the clouded brain behind his glassy eyes finally came up with after a lengthy pause was "Hmmm. I guess you do speak English."

His comment at first struck me as nothing more than a drunken non-sequitur until I realized he was attempting to focus on my red, yellow, and black jersey with the word "Germany" printed across my chest. Apparently, he had assumed I was wearing my national colors.

"Sprechen sie Deutsch?" I answered. I couldn't resist having a little fun with a brain so impaired by alcohol. My interrogator recoiled at this German response as if he had just been struck full in the face by a shot of bad breath. He then studied my person while registering expressions that passed from surprise to befuddlement to suspicion. It was with that look of suspicion on his face that his brain appeared to freeze up like a malfunctioning computer and he stood there, head lowered and tottering like a dazed bull before the matador, peering at me through his bushy eyebrows for quite some time until his wife interceded with an apologetic smile and led her brain-locked and speechless husband back into their trailer.

August 23, 2006; Day 6; Troy to Libby, Montana: No problem warming up this morning. The climb out of Troy was long and steep. We had shed our jackets before we topped the hill.

Brilliant morning sun boiled the heavy dew of last night into clouds of swirling vapor that rose from the road and grass as we followed the fast-moving Kootenai River, upstream, toward Libby. A dark cloud of worry dimmed that bright scene, however, as I felt the return of a sore thigh muscle from yesterday. I had hoped it would heal itself in the night.

Half way to Libby we met our first fellow bicycle traveler: a guy from Kansas who is on his way to Seattle on a fat-tired bike. We filled him in on what to expect when crossing the Cascades. A little rain would be nice for him to dampen the forest fires that are burning there now. Otherwise, it is so smoky he may not see much of those spectacular mountains.

The Libby Chamber of Commerce has a wireless Internet router so I tried to tap in to send some email. No luck. The signal was strong but I kept getting an error message saying my Internet Service Provider (ISP) was rejecting the emails. I'm very disappointed in the advice my ISP gave me before leaving. They assured me I could log in and send email without any trouble and it isn't turning out that way.

We started out of town toward Eureka but my thigh muscle was more painful than ever so we decided we'd get a room in Libby and rest it a day. I used the opportunity to try to solve my email problem. I found a storefront for a local ISP and hired the guy to unravel my email glitches. He worked on it with limited results. I can send text but no photos.

August 24, 2006; Day 7; Libby to Eureka, Montana: I confess I was plenty worried this morning. My strained, left thigh began hurting again and I was on the verge of despair. Without two good legs a cross-country bicyclist is like a one-winged bird – dead meat. We had rested yesterday in Libby to allow the thigh muscle to heal and it felt fine when we left town this morning but an hour into the constant up-and-downhill of today's ride it was hurting worse than ever. This despite strictly adhering to Mary's exacting regimen of 400 mg. of ibuprofen every six hours for two days and regular massage to remove the "toxins" from the muscle.

When all seemed lost, dumb luck came through for me once again. I had purchased a bottle of ibuprofen in Libby because I thought I'd lost the pills we brought from home (I'd only misplaced them). When I took a couple of the new pills about noon today my leg started feeling better within an hour. By afternoon I was pain free and stronger than ever. Mary commented that I was riding like a "raped ape" again. Call me what she will, I was ecstatic to regain my usual vigor. As for the ineffective ibuprofen we brought from home I can only guess that the drug has a shelf life that had expired.

Through much of the day, we rode along the eastern shore of Lake Kookanusa which is a handsome enough lake with clear water and forested slopes as well as the spectacular white concrete Libby Dam. Strangely, there are almost no humans to be seen in its vicinity. Until we approached the lake's northern extremity where we encountered a handful of rock climbers, we saw scarcely a soul.

We stopped and talked to a young Canadian couple who told us about their sport while one of their twin daughters held a safety rope suspending her sister high above on a vertical rock face. Across the road, another climber was shouting words of encouragement to his girlfriend as she contemplated a heart-stopping maneuver where she had to swing her body around an overhanging ledge while suspending herself by her bare hands. After several tense minutes of courage building, she made the swing and pulled herself up the side of the cliff. I shouted congratulations to her as we rode by. Mary and I assured each other that we much prefer the challenges of bike riding to rock climbing no matter how hot the air temperature and how steep the hills.

The town of Eureka is interesting. Small, it is the commercial hub of a farming valley that reminds me of the Kittitas Valley in Washington with its broad hay fields surrounded by pine-covered hills. The area is beautiful in August but locals warn us that winters are brutal. In the last few years the town has discovered the tourist dollar and the businesses that cater to farmers are being crowded out by pottery barns and book stores.

We're staying in the city park for a fee of $5, which, a sign posted in the park informs us, can be paid at the police station across the street. I walked over and paid my $5 plus a $10 deposit for which I received a key to the shower room. It seems ridiculously cheap to us but we've found tent camper fees run from $5 - $15 in these parts. For that you usually get a picnic table, a grassy plot on which to pitch your tent, access to a store, and a shower – in short, everything we need. Good deal.

Freshly showered and wearing our "evening attire" (cotton t-shirts and loose-fitting shorts,) we strolled around the corner from the city park to a little pizza parlor for our dinner. It is a homey little affair, nicely decorated with shiny, varnished pine furniture and red & white checkered tablecloths and run by a feisty woman with the entrepreneurial spirit. Years earlier she'd leased a small part of an old building on the town's main street and tried her hand at selling knick knacks which didn't pan out so she switched over to pizza and latte's and now has a profitable business. I felt glad for her hard-won success.

While Mary did our grocery shopping for tomorrow, I slipped into a book store to look for something to fill my idle moments in the evening. I settled on Saul Bellow's novel *Herzog* which comes highly recommended by literary types. We shall see.

Back at camp, with the sun now set, we settled into our tent and zipped up the sides to block out the outside world. I started reading *Herzog* by the light of my headlamp while Mary listened to a radio drama on XM satellite radio. Twenty pages into my book, I noticed Mary was softly snoring so I turned off the radio, marked my place in *Herzog* and set it aside. Just enough consciousness in me to finish this journal entryyyyyyyyyyyyzzzzzzzzzzzzzz

August 25, 2006; Day 8; Eureka to Columbia Falls, Montana: We are camped just outside of Glacier National Park in the town of Columbia Falls, Montana. Tomorrow we expect to enter the park and ride up the notoriously long and steep Going-to-the-Sun Road which takes us to 6700-ft. Logan Pass and the Continental Divide. Every cyclist we have met has advised us it is a "must do." Sitting here in town we feel like Everest climbers in base camp awaiting the final push to the summit.

Curiously, Mary has been expressing reluctance about doing the climb and has been lobbying for a less strenuous route to the south. I thought it was the steepness that concerned her but she let slip in conversation last night that something else was at the root of her apprehension: bears.

She has a long-standing fear of bears in the woods but I suspect the more immediate source was the heads-up we received from the proprietor of a convenience store several days back when he warned us that Montana is grizzly bear country. Apparently, Mary took this advice to heart and it is still on her mind. With some effort I was able to convince her that the chances of winding up in the bottom of a bear's stomach are considerably less than the chance of being run over by trucks on the highway. Now, she's worrying about trucks.

Getting here from Eureka was a mixed bag. The Old Tobacco Road out of Eureka was a peaceful stretch of road but the highway into Whitefish rivaled the Highway to Hell near Spirit Lake for sheer vehicle-induced horror. Today's dangerous stretch of road was the shorter of the two but it made up for that by so many sharp, blind curves where cars couldn't see us until the last moment. We wound up walking in the dirt through several sections out of fear for our lives. We found a long piece of yellow plastic ribbon, the type of ribbon police tie around a crime scene, along the road. I picked it up and tied it on our safety flagpole on the trailer. We now have several colored balloons, an orange strip of ribbon, the yellow ribbon, and a piece of the red and silver ribbon from a Chelan cherry orchard tied to our flagpole. Oh yeah, we both wear orange construction vests too. If anybody runs us over, it won't be because they didn't see us.

Very pretty country around Whitefish and I'm not the only one who thinks that way. There are a lot of new, big houses being built in the surrounding countryside. I was most impressed by one particular house that was built atop a sheer cliff overlooking the valley, a la the castles of Europe.

Camping near us here in Columbia Falls is a young fellow named John who is on his way to Washington, D.C. Last year he crossed the country on his bike going east to west. He says he averages about 100 miles per day which would put him in a different league of bicycle tourists (young studs) than the one we are members of (old fogies).

August 26, 2006; Day 9; Columbia Falls to Saint Mary Lake, Montana: We did it! We crossed the Continental Divide by climbing nearly 4000 ft. from Columbia Falls to the summit at Logan Pass. Mary was beaming at the summit and she deserved to. I was proud of her! Hell, I was proud of me.

They have a peculiar little system for bicycle riders in Glacier National Park. If you want to ride the Going-to-the-Sun Road you have to do it before 11:00 a.m. or after 4:00 p.m. The reason for this regulation is that the road is very popular and not very wide so they don't want any doddering bicycles gumming up the traffic flow. From what I hear, if the park rangers catch you on the highway between those hours, they'll make you get off the road and sit wherever you might be until the time is right. If they catch you cheating they'll arrest you. We actually *broke the law* for about 15 minutes until we turned into the Lake McDonald Lodge and Visitors' Center at 11:15! I'm serious, Mary was freaking out about this serious criminal activity we were involved in.

If you have to kill four hours and forty-five minutes, that wasn't a bad place to do it. We dried out our gear, napped, checked out the nifty lodge and fortified ourselves for the big climb which we were so psyched to do that we slipped out onto the road at 3:45. Fortunately, our second criminal act of the day went unnoticed by the authorities.

The mountains in this park are unlike any I've ever seen. Their sides are perfectly vertical in many cases for thousands of feet. There is a whole ridge near the pass that appears to be as thin as a knife blade while being several miles long and thousands of feet high. Apparently, this is what glaciers do to mountains. In a word – spectacular!

Our climb was a study in "slow and steady gets the job done." For most of the afternoon we were in our lowest gear, moving along at four to five M.P.H. I felt like the little locomotive that repeated over and over "I think I can, I think I can." We stopped every hour or so to eat and drink for a few minutes but the longer the rest, the more your thighs burn when you start back up so we kept the pauses short.

We met a very pretty young woman coming down as we climbed and talked to her for a while. She had begun her trek in Seattle, ridden to the summit of Logan Pass and would be heading down into Yellowstone after leaving Glacier. We thought of John from Columbia Falls and what a shame it was that the two of them didn't team up. Several other guys came zooming by us descending at unsafe speeds as we crept up the mountain. Can you imagine what would be left of a rider who crashed going down this mountain road at 40 M.P.H.? Imagine the loss of skin on the pavement not to mention broken bones. Yecch!

Even though weather near the summit was rather cool we were producing so much body heat during the climb that we were stripped down to only our mesh safety vests and shorts for the last five miles. We had to do a quick change into our fleeces within minutes of summitting. Speaking of fleece, there was a mother mountain goat with her two babies at the summit. They were so cuddly with their thick white coats and little black nubbin horns. They seemed quite unconcerned by our presence. There were also big horn sheep in the parking lot at the summit. I think they were looking for handouts.

As I was changing into some warmer clothes for our descent, a little girl with her parents in the visitor center parking lot seemed horrified that I would expose my naked chest in public. "Look at the man without a shirt!" she shrieked as if I were a man without pants. I could only wonder "Where has this child been all her life?"

The daylight was waning as we descended the eastern slopes of Logan Pass. We had our L.E.D. bike lights flashing forward and rear hoping that any passing cars would see us in the dim light. Luckily, there were not many cars at that late hour. We got to a USFS campground at Rising Sun on Saint Mary Lake at dusk and pitched our tent in the dark. Weirdo neighbors at the campground. I mean, how often do you see fifty-year-olds giggling and hanging all over each other in public? I think I was as offended as the little girl on Logan Pass.

We used our stove for only the second time on the trip to cook some Kraft Macaroni & Cheese. Tasted pretty good.

August 27, 2006; Day 10; St. Mary Lake to Cut Bank, Montana: A lodge complete with high-ceilinged dining room adjoins the Rising Sun campground where we spent last night. If the lodge is part of the distinguished chain of lodges to be found in national parks, I would have to call it modest in comparison to those I've seen elsewhere (Yellowstone and Grand Canyon being two outstanding examples) but if it is an independent, commercial establishment I would rate it quite impressive. I never did ascertain its actual status. Anyway, we had a nice breakfast there of waffles and bacon and eggs and such. Cooked breakfasts have become *de rigueur* for us since about Spirit Lake. When you're involved in fairly vigorous exercise for six or more hours per day and burning on the order of 5000 calories, I've come to agree with Mary that a hearty breakfast is warranted. "Besides," Mary is quick to remind me "breakfasts are cheap." Well, yeah, compared with supper in a fancy restaurant I suppose $15 is cheap for a meal for two. My initial response to that cost, however, is that it seems like a lot when compared to a couple of bowls of raisin bran. Mary says I'm still living in my pre-1980 bachelor world which was the last time I still bought my own food.

The service staff at the lodge had the appearance of a crew of fresh-faced college underclassmen imported from around the country to Montana for the summer season. Our particular waiter was a friendly young fellow with his mind, apparently, on other things besides our breakfast. He was long in serving the food, it was the wrong food when he brought it, and he forgot to bring us the correct food when he returned the mistaken food to the kitchen. "Other than that," Mary insisted "he was a very nice boy."

After breakfast we followed the shore of St. Mary Lake to a visitor center where one of the park rangers informed us that the detour we had planned to take into Canada from that point was nothing special so we chose to head down US 89 to the south toward the town of Browning.

"Down" is not really the appropriate preposition here because the highway started to climb immediately and steeply from Saint Mary. As we climbed it was obvious that a forest fire had denuded the hillside in the recent past. Just how recently we didn't realize until we noticed several plumes of smoke rising from various points across the valley.

Our "descent" to Browning continued to climb for several miles only to drop precipitously for several more and then climb again and then drop and then climb...... We had thought we were through with the climbing after cresting Logan Pass. Today was beginning to uncomfortably resemble yesterday. Once we left the burn area the vistas to the east were stunning: the vastness of the Great Plains. But the succession of inclines was doing a number on us. They were much shorter than yesterday's long climb but added together they were formidable.

During a snack break in a gorgeous bowl of a meadow, I pulled out our map of Montana and noticed a minor road branching off SR 89 and approaching Browning from the north. It was called "Old School Rd." and the contour intervals, as far as I could trace them on our Adventure Cycling map, showed this route to have far less climbing and descending than the highway we were following. The way we were traveling, ahead lay a long and discouraging series of hills. About 300 yards back, the way we had just come, was a turnoff that looked suspiciously like it could be Old School Rd. We backtracked to the turnoff but it bore no sign to indicate what its name might be. I wanted to take a chance and follow the road. Mary balked. She didn't like the idea of following an unnamed road out onto the vast expanse of the Great Plains. To help set her mind at ease I walked up to the only house to be seen for miles, conveniently placed at this intersection it seemed, and knocked on the door. An old man, an Indian, hair in two long braids and speaking in that somewhat slow, distinctive way that older Native Americans do, paused for a moment as if to search the far recesses of his memory when I asked him what the road in front of his house was called.

"Oh, let me see......, they call that the Old School Road. You go down that road a couple a' miles and you gonna' pass the old school." He added "Don't nobody use that school no more. Take 'em all to Browning."

I thanked him and walked back to Mary, who was holding the bicycle at the road. I thought "Wow! A real Indian." I wondered if he could be the direct descendant of one of the buffalo hunting, teepee-dwelling, scalp-taking Indians of the Great Plains. He probably was. I mean, who else would he have descended from? Maybe it's just Hollywood's romanticizing of the Indians of old but that teepee life had always seemed pretty cool to me. But as I got on the bike and we pedaled away I looked back at his starkly unadorned house against the dirt hillside. The buffalo hunts and the teepees just seemed like a load of Hollywood crap and he seemed more like a lonely, old man than a daring buffalo hunter.

Old School Road was everything we'd hoped it would be: a long, nearly straight, gradual descent that took us the back way into Browning. Best of all, Old School Road turned east, the same way the wind was blowing. For the first time on this trip, we felt the encouraging push from behind that comes with a tailwind. I was quite proud of the results my map reading skills had produced.

Browning, Montana – now there's a piece of work. I've never seen another town like it. The way we came into town we passed through a sizeable residential neighborhood of fairly modern, rather new-looking tract homes. The houses obviously had people living in them – there were cars parked in the driveways and children's toys in the yards but not one of the yards had any grass or landscaping of any type. Surrounding each of the houses was nothing but dirt – fine, dark brown silt that wind had blown against the surrounding houses until all of them had a gritty coating of native soil in every crevice and all over their new paint. They managed to be new and run-down looking at the same time. Amazing.

Browning's population, from what we saw, is predominantly Indian and many of them seem, well, depressed. I can't think of a better word to describe them. They don't talk much. They don't move much. They sure as heck don't smile much. Maybe they're happy on the inside. I hope they're happier than they appear.

Seeing no reason to tarry in Browning, we moved on toward Cut Bank. The afternoon sun was blazing when we arrived there. We immediately and single-mindedly set about procuring for ourselves a refuge out of the sun with a shower to wash the day's accumulation of salt and grit from our leathery hides. Mary's first preference was an expensive-looking motel at the west end of town. I argued for a campground our guide map mentioned. Our different preferences for the evening's accommodation have settled into a predictable pattern by now. Mary's, quite simply, is "If it makes me feel comfortable, I want it."

I tend to give considerably more weight to the cost factor than she and motels cost more than campsites so I generally favor camping.

After I had made an eloquent presentation of the relevant facts in the aforementioned debate we set off in search of the campground – I, confident we would find what we needed for a reasonable price; Mary, sullen and determined to find fault with whatever I came up with.

In its favor, the Riverview Campground had a fine view of Cut Bank Creek. It had a recreation room that included a pool table and a television, although the lack of air conditioning on a day like today made the room uninhabitable. The campground's goateed and ponytailed young proprietor proudly pointed out that not only did his campground offer a shower; it also had a sauna. I pointed out that a sauna had limited appeal when the outside air temperature was approaching 100 degrees. The cost was $20 which, while undoubtedly less than the motel, was considerable for a place to pitch a tent. The deal breaker, I decided was whether or not he could produce a patch of cool, shaded grass on which we could stretch out and read our books until the sun went down. He took me around to the far side of his main building and pointed to a single, scrawny sapling with perhaps twenty leaves spread across its several, scrawny branches. The grass beneath was a scorched, pale green.

"That's it?" I asked. "That's the best you got?" I paused briefly to consider his offer. "I guess I'll pass then."

He seemed to take offense at this. "If you're not going to pay, don't let me catch you hanging around here." He warned me.

"Right, Creepo." I thought to myself. "Like I've got nothing better to do than hang around your dusty campground."

I returned to Mary who had refused to even look at the campground. "OK, let's go to the motel" I said. Round One for Mary.

August 28, 2006; Day 11; Cut Bank to Joplin, Montana: We're stretched out, barefoot, on the cool grass in the shade of an olive tree in the town's city park. We've decided to sit out the heat of the day and perhaps push on when it cools down. It's hot today (about 90). We left Cut Bank this morning with high hopes of having our first 100-mile day but I learned from the cashier at the truck stop in Shelby that there was a computer genius in town and he was a man I had to talk to. The fact that you're reading this attests to his genius. My computer's web mail has given me no end of trouble on this trip and I haven't been able to fulfill my commitment to keep the Wenatchee World informed of the highlights of our trip. Using the cashier's instructions I found Genius' house. His mother said he was still sleeping (it was 9:00 AM). I told her I was passing through on a bicycle and desperately needed his help. She sized me up and decided my situation warranted getting Genius out of bed. He looked to be about 50 years old and is self-taught because there's no one in Shelby to teach him. Man, did he know his stuff! Got my web mail going and explained about ten other mysteries I have never understood about my computer's operation and only charged me thirty bucks.

The down side was that our little detour cost us two of the best traveling hours of the morning and forced us to pedal through most of the hot afternoon just to make the seventy miles to Chester. After swooping down out of Glacier Park onto the Great Plains we were expecting to do more. On a day as hot as today it is difficult to believe this area suffers long and frigid winters but it most assuredly does. Shelby, which we passed through this morning, is affectionately called "Shelberia" during the winter months.

This is Lewis and Clark country and it thrills me to look across the gently rolling terrain and imagine that the Corps of Discovery passed this way. We passed a monument by the side of the road today that marks the farthest north the expedition is believed to have passed. The highway (US 2) has very little traffic here, which pleases us greatly, and the shoulder is usually wide enough to give us a safe lane of travel.

A nice farm wife turned her Suburban around on the highway near Devon to stop and offer us fresh pears. She was on her way out to the family wheat harvest to feed the crew and thought we looked worthy of some of her bounty. She told us all about the family business while we greedily devoured the fruit while juice ran down our chins.

The broad, treeless expanses of Montana that are so liberating to the spirit can also be problematic to the body in a very down-to-earth way for Mary. You see, peeing is one aspect of bicycle touring that receives less attention than it deserves from the world at large. It is, of course, not uncommon for bladder pressure to build to an uncomfortable level in these wide-open spaces and for no public bathroom to be anywhere nearby. As Mary often reminds me with more than a trace of envy, this situation presents no problem at all for men. Indeed, I have been known to stop and relieve myself while straddling the bicycle just because I'm too lazy to walk a few paces off the side of the road (although I have never mastered the impressive technique of professional road-racing cyclists who are reputed to pee while seated and riding.)

Women find this very natural and necessary bodily function more problematic. When we were riding through the forest-lined highways of Idaho and Washington, squatting a discreet distance from the road behind a tree was never a problem but here in Montana the view from either direction is often unobstructed for miles and so Mary often finds herself in the vulnerable position of dropping her drawers in the open with nothing more between her modesty and passing cars than me standing watch. Should a car appear before she can complete the deed, she has given me clear instructions that it is my responsibility to shout "Car!" in time for her to abort, pull up her pants and present herself standing and fully clothed to the curious eyes in the passing cars ("Mommy, why is that woman standing in that wheat field?"). Wearing the orange construction vest doesn't help to make her inconspicuous as I have had to remind her on occasion.

P.S. We pushed on from Chester another ten miles or so to Joplin after the worst of the day's heat had passed but not before stopping at Mike's Market on the eastern outskirts of Chester. Prior to this trip I had believed the modern supermarket to be a ubiquitous feature of American life in the twenty-first century but this Northern Tier Route we are following has exposed us to an extensive corridor through the American continent where groceries are still purchased from Mom & Pops. Actually, Mike's isn't a true Mom & Pop. It's more of a hybrid – a "mini-super" to borrow an oxymoron from the Mexican vernacular.

Mike's and Chester are perfectly suited to each other. Chester has around 900 citizens and they obviously work hard to maintain their little community's amenities. While so many towns the size of Chester have fallen into decay with the rise of Big Agriculture and its replacement of human beings with monster tractors and combines, Chester is holding its own – not growing, but holding its own. And that's a good thing for Mike. If Chester were much bigger it would attract the attention of the big boys like Safeway and Mike would be squeezed out like countless other small grocers across the country.

Like the other citizens of Chester, Mike has done everything he can think of to make his place as good as he can. The market isn't big; probably twice the size of the typical modern convenience store, but Mike has worked hard to pack a full complement of groceries into its five or six aisles. The selections are much closer to what one would find in a supermarket than to the tooth-decaying, waist-expanding fare of the typical convenience store. In keeping with our times, Mike now has a deli counter and a Subway franchise as well as a row of booths for those who want to eat their recent acquisitions on-premises.

Too-hungry-to-wait was an apt description of us and we were settling into one of Mike's booths to enjoy a couple of foot-long Subway sandwiches when the man himself came over to chat with us. Easing himself into the opposite side of our booth, Mike displayed an openness about his life and business that matched his lively curiosity about our cross-country bicycle ride. He obviously relished the chance to talk to a couple of adventurers and hear about what life on the road is like. I think he envied us. I know he did. He told us that he has found his little business in Chester to be very satisfying in many ways but he sometimes dreams of getting away and seeing the rest of the world. Toward that end, he only half-jokingly offered to sell us his store. I half-seriously considered buying it. We have a definite affinity for these little Montana towns.

And now, if I might, a word about road etiquette. Anyone who regularly rides with other cyclists will tell you that there is a certain large element of our cohorts who seem to have chips on their shoulders regarding the bicycle vs. car use of the road. Cyclists are always complaining that car drivers don't give them a wide enough berth when passing. I've heard it the other way too; that cyclists need to get their butts out of the roadway according to car drivers. I've been on large organized rides where bike riders make a point of riding in the middle of the road and making cars pass them in the other lane as if they were a car. According to my cycling friends, bikes have a legal right to occupy a traffic lane. I'm going to ask the State Patrol about that some day.

As a practical matter, few bicycle riders are foolhardy enough to ride in the middle of a traffic lane even if they have the right to do so. If a paved shoulder is available, most riders will use it. If none is available, they'll hug the outside edge of the lane to give cars as much room to pass as possible. This is only common courtesy. Bicycles are very slow relative to cars and would be a considerable impediment to motorized traffic if they were to take up a lane. Fear of mutilation and death is probably a more compelling reason even than courtesy for most riders. In a collision between a car and a bicycle there can be little doubt who gets the short end of the stick.

That being our attitude, Mary and I are careful to stay out of motorized vehicles' way as much as possible. The overwhelming majority of the thousands of cars that pass us every day on the highway are driven by apparently reasonable and courteous people who are careful to put a safe distance between their vehicles and us. Most drivers, if the opposing lane is free of oncoming traffic, will pass us by moving over a lane. There are occasional exceptions, however, and the single group that most consistently "violates our space" is that of large RV drivers. So commonly do these whales on wheels pass within inches of us that if I see an RV in my rear-view mirror, I keep my eyes on it until it passes, always ready to steer our bike off the side of the road at a moment's notice if need be. From our end, it seems that RV's are often driven by complete jerks. I find this apparent breach of etiquette to be surprising because most large RV's are in fact driven by senior citizen types who have usually been around long enough to have passed through the jerk stage of life and emerge out the other end as fairly mature individuals. So why do they so often seem to be trying to run us off the road?

The most obvious way to get an answer to this question would be to ask the offenders themselves. I've never been able to catch up to one of them or I would. Failing that, Mary and I have put considerable thought into this and here's what we've come up with: Mary thinks they more or less don't see us. Either their vision is so bad that they can't resolve the image of a bicycle rider at 100 ft. or their ability to see oncoming cars is so poor that they dare not move into the passing lane out of fear that an oncoming vehicle may be there. If that is the case, I fear for the drivers of all vehicles in this country. That is a terrifying thought.

I think it is more a case of being unable to adapt to a new or unusual situation – to do some quick thinking. Passing other vehicles is an option rarely utilized by RV's either because the vehicles are not that fast or because their drivers don't like going fast. Presented with the unusual situation of having to pass when they come upon a bicycle, their old brains aren't able to accommodate the change in behavior required by the situation. Their response pattern is "locked in" by years of repetition. They simply freeze up and try to squeeze by without leaving the lane. What should they be doing? If the passing lane is free, use it. If not, there is always the option of slowing down until it is and then passing us. That particular option seems to almost never occur to drivers.

August 29, 2006: Day 13; Joplin to Chinook, Montana: In the preceding days we have heard tell of an old man traveling east in a covered wagon bound for New York. His wagon is drawn by two large horses. We caught up with him in Joplin but when we rode past his camp last night he was nowhere to be seen. Leaving Joplin this morning we crossed the highway to see if he was up and about. He wasn't. A shame, because I would have liked to talk to the fellow. He is more than likely a kindred spirit motivated by something similar to what motivates us, whatever that is. Maybe he could tell us.

Campsite of the old man we never met.

Montanans have an interesting custom. They plant small, white, iron crosses along the side of the road wherever there has been a highway fatality. If more than one person died they put a corresponding number of crosses. We saw a cluster of five crosses today at one spot – a whole family? Rarely do more than a few miles pass that you don't see a cross. It is a sober reminder that danger lurks on the highway.

Another danger that seems to be stalking Montanans is meth. There are billboards and sculptures all through this state preaching against meth use. The sculptures are one-of-a-kind creations whose theme generally is to highlight some sort of wreckage or destruction such as a rusted car or burned-out house and equate it with the damage meth does to its users.

We dropped into Havre, at 9000 inhabitants, a major population center in northern Montana. Wal Mart must think it is a city with a future because they're putting in a store, much to the distress of the existing Kmart I expect. Since the Wal Mart wasn't yet open for business we shopped at the Kmart for soap and a few things like that. We can't take on much because we have no place to put it. I had a bladder-busting blue Slurpee and a slice of pepperoni pizza while Mary went for the cheeseburger and fries. We carry most of our food, you see, in our stomachs where it can be put to immediate use.

I tested my computer's wireless connectivity at a new hotel that had apparently just opened its doors today. I was anxious to do a road test of the fix Genius did for me recently in Shelby. I sat on the concrete outside the hotel entry, my back against the side of the building, punching keys on my computer, which seemed to annoy Mary.

Something not appropriate about that in her mind. Couldn't understand what her objection was. Didn't try. Signal was on and off but I finally got an email through to Wenatchee World editor.

Arrived at Chinook about supper time and they have a campground so it looks like this is the place we'll spend the night. We cruised the town's streets for a while until we found the city park which our guide map suggested as a camping site. Couldn't find the promised (and much needed) shower so I poked my head into the nearby municipal swimming pool to see what I could find. It just so happened that today was the very day the pool closed for the season and they were covering everything up. The manager told me if we hurried we could use the pool shower.

Hoping to avoid another midnight sprinkler incident, we inquired about how to notify the authorities we would be camping in the park. As it happens, the pool manager's husband is the town cop and he looks after such things so she said she'd tell him. Hope she does.

We were eating our supper at one of the park's picnic tables when we saw a guy, unmistakably a fellow touring cyclist with his twin sets of panniers, coasting by the park and scanning the neighborhood like he was looking for something – a campground perhaps? We hailed him and he rode over. Name is Paul, about thirty and he's doing the Lewis & Clark bicycle trail which apparently intersects our route in this part of Montana. He's a history teacher and I guess he's doing a little "hands on" research for a presentation. He appears to be one of those very meticulous people who is always thoroughly prepared for any eventuality as he seemed to know every detail of his route for days to come Not particularly friendly; as soon as the useful information was exchanged he went off to the far side of the park and disappeared into his tent.

Two little blond girls eating some snacks at a nearby picnic table. Probably eight years old or so and cute as can be. They ate and talked for a while then went over to a stone chimney about ten feet high. One entered at the bottom and climbed out the top while the other dropped in the top and appeared at the bottom. Just kids exploring the world the way they did when I was one - no parental supervision required, no organized activities. It's a hard scene to reconcile with Montana's meth epidemic.

August 30, 2006; Day 13; Chinook to Hinsdale, Montana: We're camped in a cottonwood grove beside the Milk River in tiny Hinsdale (pop. 95). The locals at the store and the bar sent us down here. It's a little primitive but we have it all to ourselves except for the occasional pickup that zooms through. Local rendezvous spot?

Second flat of the day near Hinsdale

The sky looks threatening and it's windy. Rain tonight?

We saw some happy Indians near Dodson this morning. It was rather cold. We had stopped at a little roadside convenience store and were drinking some coffee and just standing around outside soaking up some morning sun and trying to get warm. Nearby, three Indians, two women and a man, were sitting by the side of the road laughing and waving at passing cars and generally having a good time. You'd think this was a good sign, wouldn't you? I mean, I did comment earlier how I rarely seem to see a smiling Indian. Well, the sad part of the story is that each of the three laughing Indians had a big can of Budweiser in his or her hand and they acted as if these were not their first cans of the morning. I can only shake my head in dismay at the sorry state of such individuals. What can be done? Excuses galore can be offered but, as with all of us, in the final analysis, each individual must take responsibility for his own progress through life.

Our first 100+-mile day! We did 110 miles and could have done more except for two flat tires. I'm rather proud of the ingenuity I used to fix the second. The best way to find the location of a tube puncture is to immerse the inflated tube in water and watch for the escaping bubbles. If you have no water, which is often the case on the highway, you run the tube near your lips to feel the stream of escaping air. Today, neither technique was doable because we got the flat in the middle of nowhere and far from any water source and there was so much wind that my poor lips never would have been able to discern a tiny stream of air from the tube against all the wind. What to do?

I'm so smart! I cut my plastic Sprite bottle in half the long way so that it formed a small water trough which I then filled with water from Mary's water bottle. I ran the tube through this to find the puncture. Even Mary was impressed.

We left the high wheat country of western Montana yesterday and dropped a little into the miles-wide Milk River valley whose principal crop is hay. The Milk River is actually a small creek so I was baffled by the size of the flood plain we are riding through until I read in some notes that accompany our map that this is the old channel of the Missouri River that was diverted by glaciers thousands of years ago. It's flat for over a hundred miles which sounds great to us who have so recently been fighting gravity in the mountains for over a week. Conditions were perfect today for covering distance: flat, cooler, nice tailwind, good road.

I should also mention that we had another reason to keep moving: mosquitoes. The water that irrigates the hay provides ideal conditions for the little buggers and they are aggressive. The tailwind that pushed us enabled them to fly right along with us. It was like a scene out of a cartoon with malicious mosquitoes just keeping pace with our ears as we sped down the road and shouting threats like "I'm gonna' suck so much blood outa' you you're gonna' collapse in a heap!" Mary had to keep slapping my back as they seemed to favor the blood from that part of my body. They are the first real bug problem we have had.

We ate our supper in the tavern in Hinsdale. Taverns, as a rule, are not my first choice for dining out but they are often the only place to get a hot meal out here on the western plain. This tavern was a scene right out of an old western movie: several dusty farmers and an Indian guy about fifty years old with their bellies up to the bar. We sat down on some bar stools near the Indian who introduced himself as Joe. He insisted on buying us each a drink which right away made me a little uncomfortable. It may have been nothing more than genuine hospitality but I don't like to step into even a casual relationship one drink in debt. Joe wanted to know all about our bicycle trip and then told us all about a canoeing trip he had just completed on the Missouri River. He got out maps to show us precisely where he had gone and went on and on about how beautiful it was. He was giving me a little more information than I really wanted about his trip but what do you do in a situation like that? Mary was concentrating on her cheeseburger and not paying much attention but I was sitting next to him and could hardly ignore him. He'd obviously had several drinks already and ordered several more as we (mostly he) talked. He seemed oddly insistent on earning the goodwill of everybody in the tavern. The farmers he engaged gave only minimal grunts and an occasional grudging smile in response to his chatter.

He must have sensed I was losing interest because eventually he switched his focus to the bartender and started talking about his book of poems which he just happened to be carrying a copy of. I thought that was a little odd. How many writers carry copies of their books when they go to a tavern? The title of his book, aptly enough, was *The Indian in the Liquor Cabinet.* He managed to drop the fact that he was a teacher at a college in Wolf Point, about a day's bike ride ahead, and then his ride showed up – a petite woman about thirty years his junior. Mary gave me a one-eyebrow-raised look that said she was probably imagining the same scenario I was: female student enraptured by older professor who has a charming side. She is willing to overlook his self-destructive alcoholism because she's going to save him from himself in spite of it. Good luck with that.

August 31, 2006; Day 14; Hinsdale to Poplar, Montana:
We cowered through last night in our little tent pitched beside the Milk River as a ferocious windstorm passed through. In the morning we had coffee at the little store with a bunch of ranchers and listened to their farm talk. They were also talking about an article on the front of the local newspaper about the verdict in a murder trial. An Indian had stabbed a Navy Seal and killed him in a bar fight in nearby Wolf Point. The farmers were surprised that the jury found him guilty of anything as the jury was mostly Indians. Sounds like there is a little racial tension around here.

Something strange *is* going on in eastern Montana. We've had at least five warnings that "you don't want to camp on the 'res'" and Poplar is in the heart of the Fort Peck Indian Reservation. The first warning we got was from farmers in western Montana and I wrote it off to a little ethnic stereotyping. Earlier today, while looking for a bicycle store in Wolf Point we were walking, by chance, near the bar where the sailor was killed and an Indian guy said to us "You don't want to go in that bar." The last two people to warn us were also Indians – one a waitress in Wolf Point and the other a policeman in Poplar. When I asked him exactly what the danger was he told me "too many crazy kids." Someone else told us about a group of river rafters who were attacked by a gang of Indian youths. Another noteworthy occurrence is that today is the first time in the 1025 miles we've covered that we have been honked at and "flipped off" by passing drivers and it happened twice. No reason – they just gave us the naughty finger.

The Indian policeman we talked to suggested we camp at the pow wow being held down by the river because they had private security there. We rode down there but it looked pretty bleak with only a few people around and little grass. I did think it interesting that the term "pow wow" is actually still used. I thought it was something that only existed in old movies. Still, why the need for so much security?

We are staying the night only because, after 107 miles today, we are too tired to pedal on to Culbertson where there is a campground. Indeed, there is no campground in Poplar and only one aging motel in which we are staying because there simply is no other safe place. The town has an inner-city ghetto ambiance with abandoned businesses everywhere and steel bars across the windows of those that remain. I don't know exactly what is ailing this community but it is not healthy.

John, the cyclist we've encountered twice already on this trip, caught up to us again today. We had just finished riding on a lengthy dirt stretch of the highway where they are repaving. The tailwind was blowing so hard along there we didn't even have to pedal. We were battling the wind for possession of our map when he rode up. He had passed us the day before only to detour to Weeping Buffalo Hot Springs off the highway while we pedaled on. We updated each other on our progress and off he went at his faster pace. We'll probably never see him again. We wished him luck. Why do they travel alone?

Crossin' Over Jordan

North Dakota, Minnesota, Iowa, Illinois

September 1, 2006; Day 15; Poplar, Montana to Williston, North Dakota: Goodbye Montana, hello North Dakota! After 667 miles of Montana we're ready for a new state, although so far the two states look a lot alike.

Joe, the talkative Indian poet we met in the Hinsdale bar a few days ago, mentioned the highway mile marker "666" which is one mile short of the Montana-North Dakota border and how it keeps getting stolen by Mark-of-the-Beast types. I'm not well informed on this subject but from what he said, those numbers have a special significance to a certain fringe element of our society who believes they have some special significance stemming from a reference to them in the Bible. Sure enough, we saw the 665 mile marker and the 667 mile marker but couldn't find the 666. No doubt it hangs on the bedroom wall of some fanatical True Believer whose fondest hope is that the world will end any day now at Armageddon.

I often think of our long bike and trailer as comparable to a semi-truck in the way it is slow to accelerate and wide in the turns. Well, as befits a semi, we pulled into the weigh station near the Montana-ND border today and got in line with the big boys. We waited patiently behind a couple of 40-ton trucks until it was our turn and then scooted our bicycle and trailer onto the enormous steel and concrete platform meant to weigh entire trucks. I expected the official behind the glass in the weighing booth to either break out laughing at the sight of us or tell us to go away and stop bothering him. He took it all in stride however, and wrote our weight on a piece of paper which he held up to the window for us to see. Our "rig" with us on it weighs 480 pounds which means we're carrying 170 lbs. in addition to our bodies. No wonder some of those hills are slow-going.

Our biking today went well – 85 miles by 3 PM. The highway shoulders in North Dakota, so far, are a great improvement on Montana's.

The weather is considerably cooler now than last week. High temperatures yesterday and today only into the 70's. A little rain today as we approached Williston.

The last fifteen miles into Williston is a series of large, rolling hills upholstered in ripened wheat and prairie grass that undulated in wind-driven waves against a sky darkened by threatening clouds as we approached the city. Television and radio broadcast towers occupy all the high ground in North Dakota and we have learned to judge where a long climb will end by looking ahead for these towers. Sure enough, once we reached the towers, it was a long descent into Williston. My guess is that many of the small communities and scattered farms are too isolated to be serviced by cable out here and still rely on old-fashioned broadcast signals for their news and entertainment. Satellite reception will probably soon end the era of tall towers – just another way life will change here in the near future.

We've been anticipating Williston for several days now as our guide map shows it as the only town between Havre, Montana and Minot, ND with a bike store. We've gone through several tires already and our inner tubes are covered with patches. The spare tube we bought in Whitefish we managed to lose and so we would be in a bad way if a tire blew and destroyed the tube with it (that's happened to us before). Imagine our disappointment when we arrived in Williston this afternoon and learned that the bike store doesn't carry the size and type of tube we need. Now we have another 130 miles to Minot where we hope they have a tube for our tires.

I think it's time to change my pants. No, I didn't get caught on a busy stretch of highway, miles from the nearest bathroom with violent intestinal cramping. I'm talking about switching my shorts for another pair altogether. Bicycle shorts are peculiar in several respects, most notably in the way they cling to the underlying anatomy and leave nothing to the imagination when, in most cases, the general public would probably prefer to be kept in the dark. The aspect of shorts I wish to discuss today, however, has to do with the padding that is sewn into them to give the rider's butt extra protection from the chafing. In anticipation of the extreme stress this extended ride would subject my posterior region to, I bought a super-duper, triple padded pair of shorts and they have admirably lived up to the manufacturer's claim of protecting me from chaffing and bruising. The problem is that I think I bought the shorts one size too big and the padding is so thick that if I don't constantly hike the shorts up by the waist, they droop and give the impression that I'm wearing a diaper – a loaded diaper.

I have been aware of this embarrassing detail for some time but have managed to rationalize by telling myself that we spend most of our time far from busy streets and no one but Mary sees me. Today, however, the reality of my sartorial inadequacy was made painfully clear to me as we were entering a burger joint in Williston. Two high school cheerleaders in those delightful little pleated skirts and sweaters they wear so well were leaving as we entered. They smiled and said hi and I smiled and puffed out my chest and did my best to look like a handsome high school athlete because, well, that's the effect pretty high school cheerleaders have on me. Always have, always will. Anyway, I was caught holding the door for about thirty seconds as several other people exited the restaurant. I heard distant giggling just as the last person cleared the door and I turned to enter. I looked toward the source of the giggle to see one of the cheerleaders pointing in the general direction of my baggy, droopy shorts. The two of them attempted to stifle their laughs when I looked their way but it was obvious they thought I looked ridiculous. In an instant I was transported back through time to my high school days when ridicule from a cheerleader, that most exalted of the female species, was worse than a death sentence. I slowly made my way inside – a broken, 56-year-old man, brought down by a specter from my past and resolved to wear a different pair of shorts from this day forward.

September 2, 2006; Day 15; Williston to New Town, ND: We thought we were tough, turning in mileages of 110/day in the last week. When we set our goal for today at New Town, which is a mere 70 miles from Williston, we questioned whether it was far enough. When we limped into New Town at 6:00 PM we had been properly humbled. It was one hill after another and, next to the Continental Divide, the hardest day of our trip so far.

One of the skills every distance rider should hone to perfection is a package of mind games to deal with adversity like the hard riding of today. The worst way to look at a hard ride is to imagine it in its entirety. That can be overwhelming. I prefer to break the task ahead into very small pieces and tell myself "I'm not going to worry about what is far ahead. I'm just going to apply myself to what is required of me in the next few minutes or half mile or to the top of this hill or whatever." That's what works for me. Mary tells me she goes about it differently. She concentrates on the song that is playing on her iPod or she thinks about something far removed from the present.

The traffic was very light on SR 1804 and the rolling hills were a bit greener than Montana's. Another difference: here the ravines are filled with trees. I'll bet it's especially colorful a little later in the year when the leaves turn. This prairie is so breathtakingly expansive and uncluttered. The abandoned farmhouses hint at a busier, more populated past to the point where I can almost hear the ghosts of long-ago children playing in their yards.

There are no towns or services for the entire 70 miles so we had to load up heavy on food and liquids which didn't help when climbing the many hills. To our right most of the day was the mighty Missouri River, considerably enhanced after its juncture with the Yellowstone near Williston, which we could often see far below us in the distance from our hilltop vantage points.

There is no campground near town so for the third night in a row we had to stay in a motel. This pleases Mary greatly and I must confess I don't mind the luxury of a bath, bed, TV, and privacy a room provides. The cost has been around $40/night which seems like a bargain. I fear I am turning into a luxury lover.

September 3, 2006; Day 17; New Town to Minot, ND:
On the road to Minot we crest a small hill and spread

before us is a lumpy blanket of ripened wheat fields mottled by the drifting shadows of scattered clouds in a soft blue sky. With no cars to crowd us to one side of this country road we luxuriate in the freedom of a full lane. A dozen pastured cows raise their heads in unison to watch us begin our silent descent. Unable to wait for gravity to pull us through the dip in the road, we pedal furiously and scatter a flock of startled ducks across the pond's surface. A warm prairie wind blows from the east but I feel a shiver of excitement cross my back as we accelerate through a turn in the road. There is no place I'd rather be. My legs are strong, my blood is racing. In my old age I will think of this day and my heart will smile and my eyes will cloud with tears at the perfection of it all.

September 4, 2006; Day 17; Minot, ND: Layover in Minot today. I forgot that today is Labor Day and a holiday. About a week ago I ordered a foldable solar panel to charge my electronic devices while we're traveling down the road and had it shipped ahead to Minot. Now we've got to wait until tomorrow to pick it up at the UPS store. We've been lying around this motel room most of the day. It was kind of nice for a while but now I'm restless to hit the road. We have worked ourselves into such a satisfying routine when we're riding. Mary agrees. Our days have the perfect blend of mystery (what lies ahead?), challenge (can we get to our goal?), stimulation (blue skies, roadside flowers, food for a hungry belly), and rewards (we pedaled all that way?!, I can't believe how fit I feel!).

My routine for each day usually ends with me propping myself up against a tree or on a picnic table and typing a journal entry into my laptop. I have received several emails from recipients of my journal dispatches that have lavishly praised my writing. These, in turn, have inspired me to devote even more time to my journal. It is deeply satisfying for me to know people are out there who enjoy what I write. I have taken it as a kind of "license to blab" as if having an audience makes me an instant expert on any and everything. This license to blab carries with it a wonderfully liberating feeling that confers a kind of power I have not previously known – not unlike, I imagine, what 007 must have felt when he first received his license to kill.

That said, I have ironically run out of things to say and will regretfully shut up and sign off.

Oh, I just thought of something!

In years to come mp3 players will no doubt be taken for granted or replaced by a superior technology. But at present my iPod is a marvelous little gadget that inspires awe in me. People have been riding bicycles across America for many years but until recently they have done so without the accompanying beat of their favorite tunes contained in a tiny device that easily fits in a shirt pocket, stores thousands of songs, and runs for many hours on its own rechargeable battery. Bicycle riding to a soundtrack turns out to be one of those exceptional syntheses that is more than the sum of its parts. For the uninitiated, the best comparison I can make is the experience of sitting in a theater watching the opening scenes of lavish movie with full orchestration. On this trip I have had the pleasure, for example, of riding along the shore of Bull Lake in Idaho while the perfectly appropriate Pastoral Symphony of Beethoven came through my earphones. I have listened, enraptured, to a pre-recorded story from NPR's *This American Life* eat up an hour of a particularly uninspiring stretch of highway between Vandalia and Tampico, Montana. But the most common and functional way we use our iPods is to let the driving beat of good, old rock 'n roll energize our tired legs at the end of a long day's ride.

There is something truly inspiring about the Stones' *Miss You* that gives new life to tired bodies. The only catch to this technique is that Mary and I each have separate iPods and if one of us is keeping time to a faster beat than the other, that person finds himself doing an inordinate share of the work.

September 5, 2006; Day 18; Minot to Esmond, ND: Well, we wasted a whole day. The folding solar panel that was supposed to be waiting for us in Minot wasn't there. We spent all of Labor Day in a motel room waiting for nothing. We also got off to a late start (9:30) on a hot day which generally is not a good idea. Even so, the flat terrain allowed us to do 100 miles which got us to tiny Esmond (pop. 159). We had our doubts about even that small population figure when we arrived at about 6 PM because we saw no sign of human life. The wild thought crossed my mind that maybe a neutron bomb had killed everybody and we, being out of touch with the rest of the world, didn't know about it. Alas, we managed to locate the town tavern, opened the door and found three living souls inside. Whew!

We were hot, hungry, and thirsty and even the tavern's toaster-ovened, frozen pizza washed down with beer tasted pretty good. The bartender, a young guy, told us he had recently moved to Esmond from California. Ya' gotta' wonder why a young guy would move to a dying little town like this to spend his days in a darkened, smoky bar. Retired people taking advantage of the cheap real estate; that's one thing but a young, working man is harder to understand. I'll bet he earns all of twenty dollars a day. He told us of several other cyclists who had stopped at the bar earlier in the summer. Always amazes me how memorable long-distance cyclists seem to be to small town people. I guess they don't get a lot of strangers in Esmond. I wonder what stories they will tell about Mary and me to the next crop of cyclists who come through town.

We camped in the city park. All through Montana and North Dakota, whenever we find ourselves in a small community at day's end we have counted on the ubiquitous town parks. Every town seems to have one. They invariably have expansive lawns and large shade trees. Many have showers. They are truly oases to the weary traveler. What makes them especially noteworthy is that a tiny hamlet with perhaps twenty houses maintains a park fit for a city of thousands. The charge for this hospitality: usually $5.00, sometimes nothing.

Darkness falls and across the town square a full moon has risen behind the huge grain elevators. In silhouette they appear to be an enormous French chateau. I sit at the bench near our tent and watch the quiet of the night in this little town. Mary is already in the tent. I can see the light of her head lamp as she reads her book. I'm not ready to quit the world yet so I walk across the square to the tavern and discover another side to quiet Esmond. Thirty or more cars have pulled up to the tavern. Scores of little old ladies get out and hobble inside. Granny alcoholics? No, Tuesday night is bingo night!

September 6, 2006; Day 19; Esmond to Pekin, ND: Our guide map has us winding our way down countless country roads toward Fargo. Nobody served a hot breakfast in Esmond so we packed up the bike and rode 24 miles to Minnewauken for our breakfast. No one serves a hot breakfast in Minnewauken either so we settled for muffins and coffee and a good helping of small-town gossip at the market. Like so many towns in farming country, Minnewauken is a dying town. The main street is mostly vacant and you don't see any children. Farming ain't what it used to be.

From Minnewauken our route passed to the south of the large but bland Devils Lake which, confusingly, adjoins the Spirit Lake Indian Reservation. The Spirit Lake Indians have exercised their special right to build a casino on Devils Lake which, today at least, appeared to be frequented by no one (unless the gamblers were spirits or pedestrians because the parking lot was empty.)

We were falling a little off the pace due to fatigue this afternoon as we climbed a slight incline outside of Tokio when Mary shouted "Dog!" with more than a little panic in her voice. Mary has a serious issue with aggressive dogs. I did a quick scan of both sides of the road and saw, a hundred yards distant, a large black and brown hound coming across an open field at full speed. Normally a modest but steady contributor to our bicycle's propulsion, Mary was suddenly putting out the horsepower of a Harley-Davidson motorcycle. I did my best to keep up with her. The pursuing hound reminded me of one of those nature videos of a lion closing in on a hapless wildebeest and we, of course, were playing the part of the wildebeest in this little drama. I did a quick calculation of our respective trajectories and determined that they would intersect about one hundred feet up the road – a calculation the hound had obviously done too because that is exactly where he was heading. I knew we could outlast our pursuer in the long run because the top of the incline was clearly visible ahead and once over the other side our wheels would give us the overwhelming advantage. The question of more immediate concern was – could we survive the *short run* with our lower limbs intact?

Our hope of escaping rested on whose endurance was greater because he obviously had the greater speed. We experienced a tense moment as he easily cleared the roadside ditch with a single bound just as we reached the point of intersection. His bared fangs snapped shut within inches of my foot as we whooshed by and I could hear his bloodthirsty snarls just behind us for several seconds, after which they faded to a safe distance. We had no problem with fatigue for the next few miles.

Old-timers gather for morning coffee in Pekin, ND.

Fatigue was again an issue about 6:00 PM when we pulled in to Pekin (pop. 80). I strode into the only establishment open in Pekin – the tavern – and was pleasantly surprised to interrupt a ladies' social in progress at the bar. Four very respectable looking women who looked like they were dressed for a PTA meeting told me all about their community's services and how to avail ourselves of them. Pekin, of course, had a large and well maintained city park in which we were welcome to camp (for free). Shower facilities in Pekin were somewhat novel: several former employees of the town's defunct nursing home had converted it into a motel/hunting lodge/public shower facility for people just like us. For $5 each they supplied us with large, fluffy towels, soap and wash cloths and ushered us into a bathroom that belonged in a suburban home.

Word of the strangers who rode into town on a long bicycle traveled quickly through Pekin. Just as dusk overtook us, a retired school teacher stopped by our campsite in the city park to invite us to have coffee and donuts in the morning with the townsfolk at the community center.

September 7, 2006; Day 20; Mile 1550; Pekin to Page, ND: The exodus of young people from the farms of North Dakota has resulted in a remarkable real estate market. A nice two-bedroom house with hardwood floors and modern conveniences on a one acre lot in neat and tidy Binford, for example, can be bought for $20,000. Our waitress this morning moved to Binford from Salem, Oregon for that very reason. A single mother of a 13-year-old son, she is studying to be a registered nurse through a state distance-learning program. Her parents bought a 100-acre farm, complete with home for $50,000.

The retired school teacher who stopped by our campsite in Pekin last night bought his house for $900! He said it would have been cheaper but the owner had just installed a new hot water heater and threatened to take the heater with him if the buyer didn't pay the full asking price.

These little towns typically have fifty to several hundred residents who live on about ten to twenty square blocks. Some have a café and small market. Most have a well-kept park and Lutheran church. The yards are mowed, the hedges are trimmed, and there are no junked cars around the houses. The surrounding countryside is rolling prairie planted in wheat, soybeans and such, dotted with small lakes and groves of trees. The catch, of course, is that you have to bring your income with you. As farmers farm more and more acres with fewer employees, jobs of all kinds disappear. One thing we've noticed is the rarity of children in these towns. Schools have had to consolidate several times over to remain viable. I can think of one class of citizens who could benefit greatly from this situation – retirees. A retiree of modest means could sell a house in high-priced America and move here to live like a king.

We kept our eyes on the eastern horizon this afternoon, watching for the world's tallest structure. I'm serious. It may be hard to believe, but the world's tallest structure stands on the North Dakota prairie – the nearest towns being Clifford (pop. 51) and Galesburg (pop. 157). It is KVLY's TV tower and at 2063 ft. it dwarfs the Empire State Building and the Sears Tower. I told you TV towers have enhanced significance in North Dakota. Alas, we saw no TV tower – just a sky full of black clouds that chased us into Page this afternoon. We arrived just in time to find the town baseball park where we stowed our gear in a gazebo as the heavens opened and soaked the town.

Damn if we didn't encounter another example of that North Dakota hospitality. We asked at the grocery store in Page (pop. 225) about camping near town and they directed us to the baseball park. Just after we got to the field a concerned citizen came down to make sure the bathrooms were unlocked for us. Just looking after a couple of strangers, North Dakota style.

We ordered some supper and ate comfortably ensconced in the town's restaurant while we watched the rain come down. As if on cue, the rain stopped about the time we finished supper and the sun came out. We walked back to the ball field and pitched our tent then took a walk around town. We can't get over how neat and tidy the houses and yards are in North Dakota – every single one of them.

September 8, 2006; Day 21; Mile 1635; Page, ND to Lee Lake, Minnesota: Awoke to a cold north wind which blew from our left side most of the day as we pedaled east. Even though it was angled so as to be only slightly opposing our progress, it made our first 25 miles exhausting. The continual howl of the wind in our ears, the buffeting caused by its surging and waning, the numbing of the fingers as it sucked the body's heat away – all combined to produce a mental fatigue that was far worse than any physical fatigue we may have felt.

Our situation improved considerably when our route turned south toward Fargo. By the time we got there the clouds had fled and what was left was a pleasant autumn day. I wanted to stop at a video store and rent the movie *Fargo* for viewing on my computer this evening but Mary does not share my sentimentality and it would be a hassle returning the DVD so I guess it ain't gonna happen. All the same, that was a great movie. I wondered if we'd recognize any of the settings as we bicycled through the area.

Mary and I called our folks from a Burger King in Fargo. They seem to be enjoying our adventure enormously by proxy. Cell phone coverage is extremely spotty in North Dakota, Fargo being a hot spot so we took advantage of the opportunity while we had it. We learned that the Wenatchee World, our hometown newspaper, ran a series of dispatches and photos I had emailed them and the folks got a big kick out of that. They get out the magnifying glass and pour over the maps every time they get an update from us.

5:00 PM found us 25 miles into Minnesota near the town of Hawly. No campground. The motel we had pinned our hopes on was closed. Our only option was to pedal another seven miles to an out-of-town campground. The campground was quite nice but we arrived very hungry and with no food. A lone box of graham crackers was the only food in the campground's tiny store other than chips and pop. Our dinner tonight: graham crackers and water.

I mentioned the campground at Lee Lake was nice – it was extraordinary. I've never seen another like it. The final approach to it was a mile of gravel road which, as you know by now, is not easy to negotiate on our skinny-tired bike. If we had had any other option we would have taken it, but, we didn't so we slowly and carefully threaded our way between the coarse gravel until we arrived at what looked like a high-class country club. It was such a paradox to see those exquisitely manicured grounds at the end of that gravel road and set as it was far from any population center. We wondered if we hadn't wandered off course. Could those golf course-like greens be a campground?

Well, sort of. We rode our bicycle around (paved roads within the facility) and marveled at the beautiful setting of lake surrounded by gently rolling, oak-covered hills. Along the shore of the lake and set amongst the trees were several hundred travel trailers. The trailers were not weekend visitors, rather, judging by the decks and covered porches and skirting attached to them, they were permanent vacation cottages that just happened to have wheels. Many had tiny lawns separated by fences and populated by elfin statuary. The whole community was litter-free and swept clean as…..well, a Minnesota town.

Oh, one other thing. We were almost killed today, the result of a miscommunication between Mary and me. Here's how it happened: We were pedaling along a four-lane highway with a nice, wide shoulder. Up ahead was the town we wanted to investigate for the night's motel and some kind of large truck on the shoulder (our side.) Because I can't see over my left shoulder very well, we have evolved a system whereby I signal Mary with the query "Clear?" and, if there are no cars coming from behind she answers "Clear." In this particular case, the left turn to the town we wanted just happened to be almost directly across from where the large truck was parked on the right shoulder of the road. Since we had just been talking about going into this town to look for the aforementioned motel, I assumed Mary understood that I wanted to cross the two lanes of traffic going in our direction to make the left turn into town. Mary, however, assumed I wanted to simply go out into the lane closest to the shoulder to pass the large truck. I asked the question, she gave the go ahead. I moved over into the far lane and heard a horn honk and tires skidding as the car behind us locked up his brakes to avoid running us over from behind. We successfully made the left turn but just barely. Close call.

September 9, 2006; Day 22; Mile 1710; Lee Lake to Battle Lake, MN: Autumn has come early to Minnesota. A gorgeous day – crisp air, brilliant blue sky. A considerable number of Minnesota's 10,000 lakes are to be found in this area with the sun sparkling on their wind-tossed surfaces today. The look of the land changed abruptly yesterday when we crossed over the Red River from North Dakota to Minnesota. Topography more rolling here and a lot more trees – true hardwood forests of oak, maple, chestnut, etc. Some handsome farms and beautiful, white churches topped by sky-piercing, needle-sharp steeples.

Having dined on nothing more than graham crackers and water the previous evening, we were impatient to find a café for a hot breakfast when we left Lee Lake. The first town on our route was Cormorant, 25 miles distant, so we took a chance and went several miles off-route to the little town of Rollag hoping it might have a source of food. Rollag had a gorgeous church and a street of handsome old houses and it even showed the after-effects of having hosted the 25th Annual Steam Tractor Celebration the week before but it had no café and its grocery store had closed for good during the last year – one more dying farm town.

Crazed with hunger by this time, we disconsolately made our way back to County Rd. 10 in a somewhat weakened state and resumed our slow progress toward Cormorant. And then a funny thing happened – we forgot all about our hunger and got caught up in the beauty of the morning and the countryside. No landscaper could ever place small lakes and hills and trees and rocks more perfectly than the ice-age glaciers did to this part of Minnesota. It was inspiring.

At noon our soaring spirits were dampened somewhat when we passed through Pelican Rapids. It appeared much of this town of 2500 population was attending a memorial service for a soldier killed in Iraq. We pedaled by the school where the service was being held with as much solemnity as possible, aware that the dead soldier's life had, in some way, made possible our lengthy and carefree jaunt through this prosperous and stable country.

Our arrival in Battle Lake at day's end illustrates how the trials of traveling often morph into its greatest moments.

We had chosen Battle Lake as our destination because it was the town closest to our goal of an 80-mile day which had a campground or motel – a motel in this case. When we arrived in Battle Lake at day's end we learned that of the two motels in town, one was full and the other was a rat hole asking $85 for a room. The owner's take-it-or-leave-it" attitude infuriated me and I convinced Mary we shouldn't submit to such highway robbery.

We repaired to the nearby Dairy Queen for some supper and time to consider our options. The outlook was bleak. We could pedal on another twenty miles to the next town or crash somewhere we probably wouldn't be appreciated in Battle Lake – showerless. Mary gets noticeably irritable when she doesn't get her afternoon shower so neither of us was happy about our situation. Out of desperation, Mary began asking the other customers if they knew of a local campground. One couple, Bob & Darlene Yaggie, after hearing the particulars of our situation, invited us to their place. Mary demurred. They insisted. I accepted. We loaded our bike into their pickup and they drove us out to their summer house on Battle Lake. Their permanent home is a farm near Breckenridge, Minnesota, and what a farm it is. Bob didn't want to sound like a braggart (he never did disclose the farm's acreage) but he is obviously proud of what he's accomplished in life and a few questions of genuine curiosity on my part about farming were all it took for him to whip out a DVD one of his kids had produced about his farm. No eight-wheeled tractors on that farm. No, he uses twelve-wheeled behemoths and he's got six of them, five state-of-the-art combines and a fleet of at least ten semi-trucks to haul his wheat, corn, soybeans, and sugar beets to market, or, rather, to a grain elevator and beet processing plant of which he is part owner.

Breakfast with the Yaggies in Battle Lake, MN.

And how did he acquire so much? He started from scratch with a few thousand dollars he had saved while in the Navy and bought a piece of land. A lot of risky but very shrewd choices later he runs a General Motors-sized farm and is still down-to-earth enough to help out a couple of stranded bicyclists at the local Dairy Queen. Where would we be without the kindness of strangers?

"Stinking and miserable by the side of the road – that's where." - Mary Carlsen

September 10, 2006; Day 23; Mile 1770; Battle Lake to Long Prairie, Minn.: In the morning, the Yaggies drove us back into town and treated us to breakfast at their favorite café – nice people.

The dominant themes of today were the headwind that has plagued us for several days and a persistent sound emanating from somewhere on our bicycle that has hounded us for the last week and is now too loud to ignore. Try as we might we cannot determine with any certainty its source. My best guess at this moment is that our rear bottom brace bearing is failing. We have located a bike repairman in Long Prairie and plan to present our perplexing problem to him tomorrow morning when he arrives at the shop. Fingers crossed.

The notorious mosquitoes of Minnesota appear to have retired for the year – we haven't seen a single one. The terrain is pockmarked with small lakes and farmers' fields. The roads are quiet farm roads and cars are few and far between. Weather is gray and windy.

The constant headwind beats one into a submission of sorts. I've noticed that I do less rubbernecking than on calmer days and, hence, I see less. To minimize our resistance to the wind, I keep hunched over and my mind tends to focus more on internally-generated thoughts than what is going on around me. Today I spent a lot of time taking stock of how I have actually experienced this trip compared with how I imagined I would. Anyone who sets off on a trip such as ours or even seriously contemplates such a trip could only do so expecting an experience that would be positive overall. Likely, there are several mental scenes the would-be traveler plays and replays like a favorite video in his head which entice him to leave the known comforts and security of home and set off on a trip in which he will encounter events of unknown nature. For me, my favorite imagined scenes were of Mary and me comfortably camped beside a mountain stream or perhaps racing effortlessly across wide open spaces. Less specific, was a general notion that we are always wondering what lies around the next bend in the road.

When trips are disappointing, that may be due to unrealistic expectations or bad luck. So far, for me, our trip has been very nearly what I imagined and therefore quite fulfilling. The part about camping by mountain streams, free of all the restrictions of civilization, has not really been realized. We have always utilized organized campgrounds or motels because showers and food are usually nearby such campgrounds and most of the land we travel through is private property and the owners don't want people squatting on their land. Besides, mountains and streams are a rarity in eastern Montana and North Dakota. Frankly, I was unrealistic about that. When I ask Mary to compare our trip so far with her pre-trip musings she says "They're similar except there were no hills to climb or headwinds to fight the way I imagined it."

A more common discrepancy that I deal with on a daily basis is my habit of focusing too much on the moment at hand at the expense of the "big picture." If one thinks of his life as a lengthy sequence of moments and the quality of one's existence as the ratio of good moments to bad/neutral moments (and that is how I think of mine) then it probably would be disappointing to tally up how much of any given day is used up by the mundane – even on a grand adventure such as ours. Relatively few times in a day do I absorb the grandeur of my surroundings or exult in the sensations of the road. If someone could tap into my mental experience in the course of a day, chances are he would find me concentrating on such unglamorous fixtures of this world as the surface of the road directly ahead (looking for sharp objects) or monitoring the strength of my legs against the miles left to go. How grand is that? How different is that from the drudgery-filled life of a worker on an assembly line? Does that sound wistful – as if I think reality should be different than it is? Because I don't. I'm just constantly intrigued by what reality is. I guess my point is that high times, like rich desserts, can only be appreciated in small helpings. Still, I am living what will almost certainly rank as one of the most memorable periods of my life and I am most definitely enjoying myself. I just want to get it on the record that even the best of times is mostly bread with a little bit of cake.

Herzog just isn't cutting it; Lord knows I've tried. I've probably read a third of that book but I tossed it anyway. I didn't like him. He's too neurotic. I have no use for such people even if he is just a fictional character. This is no time to accumulate clutter with no immediate use.

September 11, 2006; Day 24; Mile 1855; Long Prairie to Milaca, MN: As far as I know there is no name for it but *it* definitely exists: this Brotherhood of the Road, this Confederation of Cyclists. Here we are, traveling thousands of miles from home with only our own bodies for propulsion, following an obscure route which intentionally takes us far from populated centers, with limited resources, and we have reason to believe we have a serious mechanical problem with our bicycle that I can't fix. What' a guy to do?

Following a tip on our guide map that a bicycle mechanic lives in Long Prairie, I went looking for him last night. Instead of the well-appointed bicycle store I was expecting, I found a hole-in-the-wall little shop that was closed. Peering through the window into its unlit interior I could make out a few vintage, disassembled bicycles and pieces of furniture. No bicycles or bicycle accessories for sale. What I did see to partially revive my deflating spirits was a notice taped to the window informing "Thru cyclists" that help was available in the evenings and a telephone number. I called the number and left a message describing our problem then walked back to our motel and waited.

Early the next morning a guy with an accent named Jurgen called me to say he was the mechanic but he couldn't look at the bike until this evening because he has a full-time day job in another town. He suggested a friend of his might be able to help us if we didn't want to wait until evening. If my problem actually was what I suspected (bottom brace bearing) we would have to wait several additional days for the part to arrive from another city. I shuddered to think of the lost days were that to be the case so I asked if the friend could help us. Jurgen said he would give his friend a call.

Steve the Mechanic

Fifteen minutes later, at 7:30 this morning, his friend, Steve, who had just returned home from his night job as a printer, called us to say he's in the motel lobby and he's here to fix our bike. Now that's what I call room service! He took apart the bottom brace and tightened some loose parts and tweaked our shifting levers until they worked a lot better. He thinks the bearing is OK. We took the bike for a ride and it doesn't make the irksome noise. We asked him how much we owe him and he said "Nothing." No matter how I tried to force money into his hand he absolutely refused to take any. He told us he came to help us because he admires people who do what we're doing and he wants to contribute something to our success. We could only thank him profusely and wonder where we would be if not for the kindness of strangers, this Brotherhood of the Road.

We took the bike out for a trial run after he worked on it and, Wow! What a difference between how that bike handles with all our gear strapped on and as a "naked" bike. It was the difference between driving a loaded truck and a sports car. If only we could get someone to carry our gear we could cover a lot more ground each day.

Mary has found bicycling to be a great weight loss program. We haven't had access to scales to determine precisely how much weight she's lost but I must say she looks a lot better in her form-fitting bicycle shorts now than she did at the outset of our journey. By the time we get to Maine I expect she will be one hot number!

As for me, I didn't have much extra blubber to begin with so I'm pretty much down to muscle and blood, skin and bones. I must be adding some muscle to the mix though because I can pedal all day and don't get tired. Feeling great.

September 12, 2006; Day 25; Mile 1940; Milaca, Minnesota to Osceola, WI: We have tagged the western edge of Wisconsin but we're not through with mighty Minnesota yet. For the next few hundred miles we will be following the Mississippi River south and weaving back and forth between Wisconsin, Minnesota and Iowa.

World's smallest Post Office?

Ironically, today was the first "normal" day of riding we have had. By normal I mean that the wind wasn't against us or behind us nor were there any significant hills. We traveled 85 miles today and found it to be a rather easy day of riding. The reason we didn't do more was that the next sensible place to stop is 25 additional miles and 110 seemed a bit excessive.

We've been at this 25 days now and in many ways it has become a vocation. I don't mean that it has become tedious, I only mean that riding, even adventure riding, has a routine to which you adapt and we go about it purposefully. Each day we awake and set out to achieve our goal, our "assignment" if you will. We have often told ourselves that the paramount consideration is to enjoy the trip and not to knock off a certain number of miles each day. But the truth is that both things are important. I really can't say which is more important. Not getting to Bar Harbor is inconceivable to me. Short of some unavoidable disaster, I *will* make it happen. If getting there by October

10 requires some pain and sacrifice, so be it. Mary and I have had some disagreement on this issue. She thinks I push too hard sometimes.

As I was riding today I hit upon another analogy that I think nicely summarizes one key element of this ride that I enjoy. When I was in fifth grade my teacher brought to class what she called a Nativity calendar. Each day of the calendar had a hinged door behind which was a small picture of something with a Christmas theme: a wrapped gift, the Magi, a Christmas ornament, etc. Each day a student who had distinguished himself in some way on the previous day was allowed to open the day's "door" and reveal the secret behind it. In retrospect it seems like a trivial affair to discover the mystery behind each door but to me it was a much anticipated event. That is how I feel about each day's ride. I look over the map at the names of the towns through which we will pass. Towns with names like Dalbo, Stark, Sunrise and wonder what they will be like. What kind of people will we meet? What unexpected things will happen?

We were walking to dinner at Subway tonight at the far end of town and we had to scurry across a street to beat the oncoming traffic. I mentally noted how light on my feet I feel these days. I felt like a kid just let out to recess and wanted to keep on running. I haven't felt that way for years. It's not just that I'm obviously in better shape; there is an excitement that permeates our days. Mary feels it too. There is more cooperation and less head butting between us than usual. She sure can be sweet when she isn't pissed off and she hasn't been pissed off in days. I like her so much sometimes I want to take her hand and skip down the sidewalk. I think these *are* the best of times.

It's too bad no one will pay me to do this. I think I could learn to like this job.

September 13, 2006; Day 26; Mile 2040; Osceola, WI to Red Wing, Minnesota: We made a big change today. We mailed the trailer and all the camping gear home and will be staying in motels from now on. Several things contributed to the decision but I think the primary reason was that short ride we took on the bike without the trailer in Long Prairie. We both felt so liberated to not be pulling that thing! We haven't been able to get that release from bondage out of our minds. Also, I was reading the guide map's description of the next two hundred miles and they were talking about all the steep hills and it occurred to me that our riding would be a lot more pleasant without an anchor around our necks in the form of that trailer. We're 50 pounds lighter now and one wheel shorter. Amazing how readily Mary parted with so many of her "necessities." Our remaining possessions are now in the two small saddlebags and two smaller accessory bags.

It has not escaped my attention that surrendering the trailer represents the culmination of a difference of opinion between Mary and me that has been a source of friction throughout this ride – and Mary's opinion has prevailed. She has always argued for luxury over frugality, for king size beds over sleeping bags and a star-filled sky. Ironically, it was I who actually suggested we send the trailer home as we rode along the bluffs above the Mississippi this morning. We have stayed in motels for the last few nights because there haven't been any campgrounds. Is this what we can expect as we move further east? If we can't use the camping gear it seems pointless to have it drag us down. But there is another change that has happened – a mental one. When we planned this trip we talked as if we would be camping most of the time and spending perhaps one or two days a week in motels. That's not the way things have worked out. Mary's constant pressure to go the motel route has worn me down and overcome much of my penny-pinching nature. Rather than fight her each evening over where to spend the night I have resigned myself to letting her have her way. Frugality has always been instinctive with me; it is a way of life that has served me well in the many years when money-making was not a top priority. But we both earn comfortable livings these days and we actually have some money in the bank. We can afford motels. The change of mind that has occurred is that I now say to myself "If what we're doing now doesn't justify spending some money, what would?" and I can't think of anything better.

We saw a UPS truck making a delivery just after we had crossed the river into Stillwater and asked the driver where a UPS store might be. He pointed to a hardware store on the corner that serves that purpose for the citizens of Stillwater so we unfurled our tent and bags in the parking lot to dry them while I disassembled the trailer and then turned it all over to the store clerk for shipping. I got a little sentimental when I packed our no-longer-needed items. It was like saying goodbye to old friends. They have served us well and I appreciate that. Sentimental fool that I am.

Three weeks of traveling have made it quite clear what is truly necessary in the way of accoutrements and clothing for a trip such as this. Weight reduction has been a powerful incentive to shave extra pounds of unnecessary gear and Mary is amazed at how little she requires and even I am a little surprised. When planning for this trip we both assumed, for example, we would need a minimum of three pairs of bicycle shorts and jerseys and now we find ourselves content with one each which Mary rinses out each night (I'm a little less regular with the rinsing. I would like to think it's because I don't sweat much but Mary insists it's because I'm immune to my own odor). My total wardrobe now consists of: a windbreaker jacket, a fleece sweater, one pair of biking shorts, one biking jersey, one pair fleece gloves, one bathing suit/shorts with net underwear, one cotton T-shirt, one pair running shoes. All of these items plus my laptop computer can be comfortably stuffed into my pannier which occupies about the same amount of space as a basketball. All of my miscellaneous gadgets and valuables like my camera, wallet, headlamp, etc. fit into an accessory bag about the size of a volleyball which straps on the bike's front rack. The same for Mary. Take those few items away and we're just two naked people on a bicycle in the middle of America.

While ridding ourselves of so much today, we acquired something new. It had really become *too much* to be chased from farmhouse to farmhouse like a couple of cowardly intruders by those ill-mannered dogs. My peace-loving nature could only handle a finite amount of humiliation at the fangs of those bullies, so, after careful consideration, I think we have come up with a reasonable and humane solution to the "dog problem" – sulfuric acid. No, just kidding. Seriously though, we bought a BB pistol at Wal Mart in Stillwater. I think it will get the job done just fine without leaving a trail of horribly burned or blinded dogs in our wake. Having stopped an errant BB or two in my youth, I know that unless they hit you in a particularly tender spot like an eye, lip or scrotum, BB's might leave a small welt but they're not going to do any lasting damage. At least that's true of a boy in blue jeans which I assume is roughly comparable to a dog with an average coat of hair. We've had a few more close calls since the Hound of Tokio gave chase a week ago. Mary takes their barking, snarling and chasing seriously but I think it's all just good sport to them and no harm is intended. Of course there is always that one bad apple that would latch onto your leg and bring you down on the asphalt, so I got the pistol. I think a well placed BB would probably be all it would take to teach them a little respect. We will probably be doing everyone, including the dog, a favor by pinging our canine pursuers. A dog that runs into the street after things is going to get hit sooner or later by a car.

Our route is along either side of the Mississippi River now and the enormous barges moving upstream are impressively large. I always enjoy watching the wheels of commerce turning. Red Wing, the home of the shoe company, is an interesting town and where we'll spend the night. The downtown, which is quite large, looks like a movie set from the 1930's – lots of three- and four-story brick buildings and various other old-time architecture. I keep expecting James Cagney to come screeching around the corner in a '35 Ford with a Thompson submachine gun blazing out the window. There are lots of old mills and factory buildings along the river's edge which have been vacated by industry and filled with boutiques and restaurants to make it a friendly looking place. Tonight we shall dine on a Godfather's Pizza in one of them.

September 14, 2006; Day 27; Mile 2135; Red Wing, MN to La Cross, WI: Talk about not seeing the forest for the trees! I just realized that several days ago we passed within ten miles of the biggest city in Minnesota – Minneapolis – and never knew it. When we rode south from Stillwater we were practically in a suburb of the Twin Cities. The reason is the unique nature of our Adventure Cycling maps. They break the route down to small pieces which is great for seeing lots of detail but a lot like walking around looking at the world with a microscope attached to your face – you see what you are looking directly at in great detail but you're likely to miss anything out of your direct line of sight. We need to acquire state maps when we cross into a state so we have some idea where we are in this world relative to the rest of it.

 Our guide map apparently assumes that cyclists abhor traffic above all else and goes to great pains to route us around busy highways. In our case, there is something we abhor more than traffic – steep hills. The prescribed route had us climbing in and out of the Mississippi River valley all day. The bluffs on either side of the river are quite steep so this was no small matter. We chose to follow US 61 which stays right along the river and is almost perfectly flat. The irony is that the traffic wasn't that bad. The incessant whiz and zoom of passing cars can really scramble the brain at times but this relatively light traffic didn't bother me at all. There was one small price to be paid for our clever rerouting, however. We were rolling merrily along US 61 when it suddenly became I-90 without warning. There was no choice to be made – just big signs warning that it was ILLEGAL TO RIDE A BICYCLE ON A CONTROLLED-ACCESS HIGHWAY! Mary freaked out, of course. We were breaking a rule! My attitude was, hey, we'll just ride on the freeway until there's an off-ramp. It's not our fault we're here. We wound up carrying the bike over a few guard rails and through a field or two of knee-high grass until we found a "legal" road.

The Mississippi River is so massive that the breeze that blows to shore is cool and moist as an ocean breeze and it kept us cool all through the warm afternoon. We stopped and talked with a couple of professional woodcarvers – very talented guys. The guy who owned the shop was showing us some of his stuff when another guy showed up. He showed great deference toward the shop owner and I gathered through his comments that he was an amateur who had just started carving the year before and had really only completed one carving – which he had in the trunk of his car and wanted the shop owner to come out and see. I walked out with them expecting to see something amateurish but what I saw blew me away. He had carved a hawk that was so realistic I had trouble believing it was wood and not feathers and flesh! That guy's got a future.

"Amateur" woodcarver and his hawk in Minneiska, MN.

We did 95 miles and could have done more but this is where the motels are and we're utterly dependent on them now that our camping gear is on its way back to Chelan. Our chosen destination was La Crescent but there are no hotels in that town (we learned upon arrival) so we had to pedal to La Crosse on the Wisconsin side of the river where we found: 1) an inexpensive motel that Mary wouldn't stay at because she called it a "hooker hangout" 2) several others that were booked full 3) some $100+ places that were a little too hoity toity for my wallet. We settled on a $102 + tax room at the Holiday Inn. When we got rid of the tent I was remembering the $35 - $40 Mom & Pop cabins in Montana and North Dakota. I hope these prices don't presage a trend in the eastern half of the country.

The uncertainty of riding toward a town with a motel of unknown price, quality or availability has proved disconcerting. We tried something new this evening. We looked down the road to our destination and Googled it where we found a bed & breakfast that looked nice and reasonable and made reservations. We'll see how that works out.

September 16, 2006; Day 29; Mile 2275; La Crosse, WI to Dyersville, Iowa: A ferocious wind battled us to a standstill in Dyersville after only 40 miles today. I shouldn't say we couldn't have gone farther but the 110 miles required to reach the next town with a motel seemed beyond us in the face of such a headwind. Not that we need an excuse for crapping out and idling away most of a day here, but if we did, I should bring to the reader's attention that Dyersville is a town of 4035 residents and several distinctions: it was the location of the Kevin Costner movie "Field of Dreams"; it has a church large enough and grand enough for a European capital city (the Basilica of St. Francis Xavier); and, of greatest interest to me, it is the home of the National Farm Toy Museum.

I learned of the toy museum from a brochure that was tucked away in the drawer of our motel room's desk. Here was welcome news indeed. Instead of watching reruns on

TV or leafing through the classified ads of a cast-off newspaper to pass the time, we could visit a toy museum! It sounded like a splendid way to spend an afternoon and I told Mary of our good fortune with considerable excitement in my voice. She was sitting on the bed reading her book and at first she showed no sign of having heard me. "Did you hear me?" I said. "They have a museum of farm toys in this town." To this she slowly lowered her book, turned her head toward me and peered over the top of her reading glasses with a look that said "So?" My heart sank, for without even uttering a single word she had managed to convey to me her complete lack of interest in, what to me, was a serendipitous find indeed. I had been through this situation before – a situation in which Mary makes it clear that she thinks there are two kinds of people in this world: nerds like me who have never outgrown their boyish fascinations and normal people like her. Experience had taught me that there was no way I was going to persuade her to appreciate a collection of farm toys and so, after one or two more feeble attempts I gave up and set off in search of the museum, leaving her to her novel.

The National Farm Toy Museum was just a couple of blocks down the road from our motel, housed in a metal building that, appropriately enough, could pass for a large maintenance barn on one of the giant Iowa corn farms we had ridden by that day. The museum's entrance was a small gift shop staffed by a young woman who looked totally bored with her job and that was easy enough to understand because there were only a handful of cars in the parking lot and no one other than she and I in the gift shop. The only other visitors besides me in the museum itself were several old guys who, I imagined, had themselves grown up on farms and had experienced firsthand what the museum sought to portray. From time to time, one of them would point out something in one of the museum's many tableaux of farm life, chuckle, and relate a story from his youth. As I watched their rickety progress from display to display, I couldn't help but realize that a few hours work from a skilled taxidermist and *they* would make suitable exhibits. If we had learned anything from our passage through agricultural America on this ride, we had learned that the small family farm as portrayed in this museum and lived by these old men is a disappearing phenomenon and while I realize this change is the result of free choices and economic realities, I can't help but lament the loss.

The museum's salient exhibit is the toy model tractor. They have thousands of them in all shapes and sizes. I never realized how popular toy tractors have been over the last hundred years. But for me the highlight of the exhibits was a 1960's vintage Happy Time tin barn. It was the exact model I got for Christmas when I was ten – complete with silo and farm animals. One could make the case that I have so enjoyed this ride through thousands of miles of farm country because of that tin barn from my boyhood. How many hours I rearranged my cows and pigs and putted my tractor up the ramp into that tin barn! Each stone and board stamped into its metal walls had fascinated me as a boy and as I once again looked at it through the glass of the display case, it transported me back to that Christmas morning long ago. It was my best Christmas ever.

(Note to the reader: No journal entry was made for September 15 so this entry combines two days: 9/15/06 and 9/16/06.) In reference to my journal entry of September 14, our first experience with a bed & breakfast was quite positive. The Elkader B&B is an elegant and large old Victorian house in Elkader, Iowa run by a very hospitable couple (the McConnells) who were so impressed to have cross-country cyclists as guests that they upgraded us to the master suite and plied us with drinks and attentiveness from the moment we arrived. I had told Mrs. McConnell we were cyclists when I made the reservations but she had interpreted that to mean *motorcyclists*. When I announced who I was at her front door, standing in all my glory in my cycling tights, she looked me up and down and said "You came from where?" Once they realized we weren't a couple of leather-clad ruffians mounted atop Harley's they went out of their way to make our stay enjoyable, including a superb breakfast of French toast with fresh strawberries and *real* whipped cream. We'll have to do that again when we get the chance.

On the other end of the spectrum was a café in Harper's Ferry, Iowa where we ate lunch yesterday. The place was empty when we arrived. I suppose it was the café host's wrinkled and unwashed trousers, worn in the about-to-fall-to-earth style of today's hip-hop urban youth that first caught my attention. The friendly young man who greeted us called himself Romel and disclosed he is an immigrant from India in answer to a query from me. He told us he had recently purchased the café at a bargain price and it soon became clear that his business philosophy was "success through low-overhead." Romel had no employees. He was the cook/cashier/dishwasher/maitre d'/waiter all in one.

Our lunch began on a thirsty note. The American café custom of serving customers a complimentary glass of ice water upon arrival is apparently not observed in India. I don't mean to say that Romel was rude or uncaring because he was quite talkative and pleasant to a fault but after ten minutes of chatter and no water I slipped in a request. He went into the kitchen and returned with a glass of tepid tap water – for me. There was none for Mary.

When another couple arrived and ordered a root beer and Dr. Pepper they were told those particular beverages were not available even though they were both featured on the printed menu. The woman ordered a salad and Romel returned with a plate of lettuce – only lettuce. The woman asked for "some tomatoes or something" whereupon Romel returned with one sliced tomato. When we paid our bill I saw that the till had several one dollar bills, one five and one ten in it – nothing more. Far be it from me to lecture others on the finer points of restaurant etiquette (and, in fact, that was the exact gist of Mary's comments to me when I mentioned Romel's shortcomings as a restaurateur) but the poor guy had about as much chance of making a go of that café as I would as I would as a funeral director.

When we turned away from the river valley to climb through the limestone cliffs at Marquette after our Spartan lunch at Harper's Ferry, we were expecting a nasty climb. Our maps are color-coded for elevation change and the road from Marquette to Monona went through several color changes. But climbs like that are where we really reap the reward for sending that trailer back home. We were literally at the top before we realized it. We kept waiting for the rest of the hill to come along and it never did.

One thing that I learned from the roadside cuts on that ride is the amazing fact that the fertile cornfields in this part of Iowa are a thin veneer of topsoil over a bedrock of limestone that is hundreds, if not thousands of feet thick. Who'd a' thunk it? It looks like peanut butter spread on white bread but the corn loves it. Never saw taller corn.

A strong headwind kicked up about ten miles out of Elkader. I got down on my aerobar and we kept up a steady twelve to thirteen M.P.H. which is not that much less than our usual fifteen or sixteen in calm air.

Conditions like those are where our tandem really shows its stuff.

September 17, 2006; Day 30; Mile 2360; Dyersville to Muscatine, Iowa: For thirty days we have avoided rain on this trip but it caught us today. Not bad though – about thirty minutes worth as we pedaled into Muscatine this afternoon. You better believe we'll be watching the Weather Channel tonight. They say farmers know the weather but long-distance bike riders pay close attention too. Wind and rain and heat and cold can make a big difference in the day's ride. I'd say we watch the Weather Channel more than any other when we get to our motel room.

Studying maps is an important pastime too. Every evening and several times during the day I study my maps like a general preparing for battle. Our Adventure Cycling maps have us hopping from one county road to another at least ten times a day. On these back roads finding a grocery store or café can sometimes be a challenge and the maps help with that.

We left Dyersville at 6:45 AM and nothing was open. We couldn't find a café for breakfast for the first thirty miles and hoped the town of Wyoming would have one. It didn't but we found something better. It just so happened they had their annual firemen's pancake breakfast this morning and it was going strong just as we rolled through town. I think we got our five bucks worth. Mary and I both went back for seconds and thirds: pancakes, sausage, eggs, hash browns, orange juice and coffee. The fire station was filled with lively chatter. The town of Wyoming itself is probably home to no more than a hundred people while this breakfast attracted several times that number. Obviously, these people form a close-knit community. Mary and I were probably the only two people in the place who didn't know everyone else but that didn't stop the locals from treating us like family.

Mary gets her $5 worth at Fireman's Pancake Breakfast in Wyoming, Iowa

Iowa makes another state where we haven't met any long-distance cyclists. We met only one in North Dakota and none in Minnesota. Perhaps it's too late in the season although we think it the perfect time to travel. Our weather has been quite good and we're hoping for great autumn colors in the Northeast. Even though we don't see many cyclists, locals we talk to seem to have keen memories for other cyclists who have passed through. I suppose they don't get many outsiders in these rural areas and when they do they tend to remember them.

Muscatine is on the Mississippi River and tomorrow morning we'll cross and enter Illinois. This is a milestone that anyone using the Adventure Cycling Northern Tier maps would understand. Muscatine marks the end of Section 7 so it's a place name we've spoken often. Long after the vast majority of town names are forgotten we will still remember the names of those that marked the beginning and end of sections – names like Dalbo, Stillwater, Fargo, Cut Bank, and Minot. They may not be very significant towns to most of our fellow countrymen but they're special to us.

I was holding the bike outside of Muscatine's Super 8 motel while Mary checked in when a guy walked up to me and started chatting about our bike and our ride. He asked me if I knew who Bob Breedlove was and I told him I didn't.

"Only the greatest long-distance tandem bike racer of all time" he told me. He went on to tell me that Dr. Bob Breedlove was a native Iowan who had been killed the previous summer in the Race Across America after a stellar career as a bike racer and orthopedic surgeon. The circumstances of his death are disputed but the official Colorado State Patrol version is that Breedlove, who was riding a single bike, slumped over the handlebars of his bike while riding on a lonely Colorado highway, crossed the center line and collided with a pickup truck. The autopsy determined that Breedlove showed no sign of having had a heart attack or stroke and had no drugs in his body. He was known to be a very safety-conscious rider. Several years earlier he had set a world record by crossing the United States on a tandem bike in a little over six days.

"Six days?" I said, trying to recall how far we had come in the last six days. No, I'd never heard of Dr. Bob Breedlove but he sounds like one hell of a guy. Six days to cross America on a bicycle – *yikes*!

September 18, 2006; Day 31; Mile 2488; Muscatine, Iowa to Henry, Illinois: A person could get the wrong idea about cycling on a day like today – flat ground and tailwinds. I know how sailors of old must have felt when they caught a good wind. The spirits do soar on such occasions! We covered 128 miles today and there were times when the wind was pushing us so forcefully that we were going 30 mph on flat ground. On one long stretch at the end of the day I yelled back to Mary as we streaked past a corn field like a rifle bullet "Why haven't any cars passed us?" No answer from Mary so I yelled the answer "Because they can't!" More tailwinds and fair weather forecasted for tomorrow. I'm already making plans for another record-breaking day.

Before starting on this trip we were confident that we would be doing one hundred or more miles per day with relative ease once we found our stride but it hasn't really turned out that way. We have had a few exceptional days where we have cracked the 100-mile barrier but not often. One reason we thought that is that we rode more than 100 miles in a day on quite a few occasions on organized rides such as the Seattle to Portland ride and we weren't as fit then as we are now. Interestingly, when we compare statistics with other touring cyclists we find that we are actually *above* average in our miles per day. So what's up? Why the discrepancy?

There are riders who average a hundred – John, whom we met in Columbia Falls, Montana was one. They tend to be young men and traveling alone, which helps. You make a lot more stops when you ride with others because everybody stops for everybody else which adds up to more total stops. Probably the biggest thing that slows you down, though, is baggage. There's a big difference between riding a stripped-down racing bike on a day ride and a touring bike with its bulging complement of panniers. That distinction was made abundantly clear to us when we road tested our unencumbered bike after the mechanic in Long Prairie worked on it. It was much faster than the bike we ride everyday. There is also the "day after" effect. When we rode the 200 miles of the Seattle to Portland ride in one day we didn't get up and do it again the next day – we didn't get up period. You can put a lot more into a day's ride if you know that day's end is going to be followed by a week's recovery. We figure we're averaging about 80 miles per day and that's not too shabby.

We finally met another long distance cyclist – at our hotel in Muscatine. He was a 77- year-old guy who was pedaling 700 miles to his 60th high school reunion! At 55 and 56 years, Mary and I felt like whippersnappers.

So many dead raccoons on the road! We must see fifty or more every day. Hit by cars, they assume such gruesome poses in death I can't help wondering if they died in as much pain as their expressions suggest. Coons and cornfields are a deadly combination and Iowa and Illinois sure do have the corn. Here in Illinois it sometimes seems we are in a forest when the corn on either side of a narrow country road is ten to twelve feet high. Speaking of raccoons – we really need to spend a little time in the sun without our bike helmets and sunglasses on. We both have a bad case of "raccoon eyes" and Mary has a white chin strap where her helmet strap shades her skin (I have a beard so mine doesn't show).

Mary on the Mississippi River Bridge at Muscatine, Iowa

It has been my experience that the considerable resources required to build a bridge across a major river like the Mississippi are allocated only when there exist substantial economic reasons to travel from one bank of the river to the other side, i.e., usually two cities separated by the river. While Muscatine might qualify as a large town or even a small city with a population of 23,000, there is no city, no town, indeed, not a single house on the Illinois side of the river opposite Muscatine and yet there is a bridge here. Talk about a waste of tax money! We had girded ourselves for the usual peril the bicyclist faces when crossing bridges with their steel-grate decking and lack of bicycle lanes but we were pleasantly surprised and more than a little shocked to encounter none of the usual hazards on the bridge at Muscatine. This is because we didn't encounter a single car on the bridge. This despite stopping for a leisurely photo shoot of Mary straddling our bike with the

Mississippi and Muscatine in the background. This bridge is not new but even in the distant past when it was built it had to cost millions of dollars – go figure? No doubt its disuse is why Adventure Cycling chose it as the point of crossing. I guess the taxpayers of Iowa and Illinois are the ones who should be grumbling – not a bicyclist from Washington who got a free, safe ride over the Mississippi, eh?

In the same way Montana and North Dakota were endless wheat fields, this part of Illinois is endless corn fields. We have been riding for 2500 miles almost exclusively through farm land – 2500 miles! I guess you could say this is the hard way to get some feel for how much America's farmers produce.

We crossed the Spoon River today. I seem to remember a "Spoon River Anthology" by one Edgar Lee Masters from my high school literature textbook. It was a collection of epitaphs for the citizens of one town and my impression as a teenager was that they were a sorry lot on the whole. I'll have to go back and read them some day as an adult and see if my outlook has changed over the years. Could this be *that* Spoon River? Not to be confused with Henri Mancini's "Moon River," of course. Where is that?

September 19, 2006; Day 32; Miles 2606; Henry to Watseka, Illinois: Another great day of "sailing" across the Illinois plain. 116 miles today. Winds from the west 10-20 mph. As we are traveling east this was a good thing. Besides, we needed a little help. Since we mailed our camping gear back home we have to find a motel each night and the only available one was 116 miles from where we stayed last night. This may seem hard to believe but the situation is this: our route intentionally stays away from towns of any size so as to minimize traffic. Consequently, motels are few and far between. I'm dreading the day we hit rough weather and can't make the distance. We'll be huddling beside the road, shivering and waiting for the dawn.

Our route may be following minor roads with light vehicle traffic but there is no way to traverse northern Illinois and not cross several busy Interstate highways. We crossed three of them today (I-39, I-55, I-57). As if we are flotsam in the calm water above a waterfall, one gets the sense when crossing these endless streams of cars and trucks that we are nearing the event horizon of some enormous entity to the north that is pulling everything in this vicinity toward itself. That entity is the urban behemoth, Chicago, a mere 40 miles distant, which dominates this part of the state like a black hole at the center of a galaxy. We pause only briefly on the overpasses to marvel at this sight of commerce-in-motion and then hurry on our way lest we, too, are sucked into the current and swept toward the city.

We had breakfast in Henry at a little café right where a big green bridge crosses the Illinois River. Good breakfast and another entrepreneurial success story: woman turns old house into café, serves good food for a reasonable price, makes a decent living and provides community with valuable service in so doing. Just the kind of story I love to hear. That's the kind of world I want this to be.

We had stopped miles from any town to drink some Gatorade and check our map. I turned from the highway and walked a few paces toward a cornfield intending to pee when I heard a growl. Twenty feet from me, curled up and lying in a ditch amongst the tall grass was a large, brown and white dog. I moved closer, thinking it might be injured and it growled again. I couldn't imagine what a dog was doing out there, far from any town or farmhouse. The only plausible scenario I could imagine was that it had been hit by a car and immobilized so I moved yet closer. It disproved that supposition by getting up and retreating to a culvert that crossed under the highway from which it continued to growl at me. Realizing the dog clearly wanted nothing to do with me I left it alone but never did think of a good explanation for its behavior. Dogs don't live in the middle of nowhere. They attach themselves to humans one way or another, yet there was no evidence that any person had recently visited that area. The story of Grayfriars Bobby came to mind, about the dog whose master died and Bobby stayed by his gravesite, day and night, for the rest of its life. Townspeople brought food to that dog. But there were no footprints or tire tracks to indicate that anyone came to visit this dog. I wonder what will become of it.

Chicken, pig, or cow?

Speaking of dogs, since we got the "protection" no dogs have tried to bite us. I'm a little disappointed as I have been looking forward to dispensing a little "frontier justice." Two black mutts took up the chase today and I had my BB pistol drawn and ready to fire but it soon became clear that they were just running along side us for the fun of it. No barking, no growling, no bared teeth. I've had to content myself with taking occasional shots at road signs for target practice.

Something peculiar we have noticed is that farm animals seem to be fascinated by us, especially cows. Horses, sheep, goats and cows all stop whatever they are doing when we pass by and stare at us, en masse, as if we were the strangest thing to ever come their way. It is quite a sight to see an entire herd of cows stop their grazing and lift their heads to watch us pass by. Pigs are the exception. They totally ignore us.

Speaking of farm animals, Mary and I have taken to playing a little game as we move through the countryside. Quite often, especially if there is a headwind, we are given advance notice of which animals can be found at the farm up the road by our sense of smell. Barnyard manures are species-specific and we often challenge each other to make the call: cow? Horse? Chicken? And most dreaded of all – pig? Mary professes to find each of them disgusting in their own way but I must admit to a certain fondness for the smell of cow droppings. Horse manure isn't bad either.

It has happened again. For the umpteenth time, some guy asked us today if I did all the work and Mary just came along for the ride. He asked in jest, as they always do, but what is it about the American psyche that so often comes up with this question/accusation of sloth on the part of the stoker when they see a tandem bicycle? Are they confusing a tandem with one of those pedicabs like they had in Vietnam where the passengers sit in a carriage seat and the driver pedals out front? Mary has heard this line so often she is starting to take offense and she's taking that offense out on me. She thinks I should step forward and defend her honor with a hearty endorsement of her as a tireless stoker. I tell her there is no point making an issue of a little light-hearted jest.

To begin with, one thing many people don't understand about a tandem bike is that both sets of pedals must turn at the same speed because they are connected by the chain that transmits the force of my pedaling through her sprocket to the back wheel. If I pedal, she *has to* pedal at the same speed. She can't just coast while I pedal. Of course, there is nothing to say she has to pedal with any particular amount of effort, and, in fact, there is no way for me to know with any precision how much effort she is expending. She has demonstrated on a few occasions what it would feel like to me if she weren't pedaling at all by removing her feet from her pedals and allowing me to do all the work. It's definitely harder for me when she does that. Still, I couldn't say if she's contributing 50% of what I do or 90%. I don't expect her contribution to equal mine because I'm bigger and stronger and for that matter I weigh more so I should contribute more. They do make a special rear hub for bicycles that incorporates a strain gauge and thereby gives the rider a digital readout of the precise power output, in watts, at any given moment. Such a device would allow us to answer this question once and for all by noting our power output when both of us are pedaling and then noting it when only one of us is pedaling. The reason we don't have one of those devices is that they cost $1000 and it's not worth that much to me to find out.

I do remember one time when we were climbing a steep mountain pass and discussing something as we climbed. It suddenly dawned on me that there was something lopsided about our conversation. Mary was blabbing away in full sentences while I, in return, was only able to reply with short, one-word answers because I was so out of breath. On that occasion I had serious doubts that she was doing her share of the work. But I think that climb was an exception. The bottom line for me is that whatever she's doing back there, we make our miles each day, so it's enough.

East of Eden

Indiana to Maine

September 20, 2006; Day 33; Mile 2736; Watseka, Illinois to Wabash, Indiana: Another stellar day for making miles – 130 of them, only today we had to earn our progress as we had very little assistance from the wind. Again, we had to push ourselves a little beyond what we would have preferred in order to make it to a town with a motel. When we got to Wabash we discovered that our preferred hotel was booked solid so we raced across town to the only other one – the Wabash Inn. Let's be frank, it's an overpriced dump but we're happy just to have a room. The night is cold and we have no other place to go.

In three days we have crossed Illinois and more than half of Indiana – 375 miles. I'm feeling comfortable that we now have some "cushion" should we have trouble down the line and not be able to do the requisite 70 miles per day. We should still be able to get to Bar Harbor by October 10. I wouldn't say central Illinois is boring but two days of it were enough for me. Indiana has a little more varied topography and around Wabash we passed through some nice countryside with rolling hills and valleys filled with oak and walnut trees. The roads we travel have almost no traffic and could best be described as paved bike paths. They're meant to be wide enough for an occasional tractor but that's perfect for bicycles.

Did you know pigs eat grass? I didn't, but we saw a field full of them. They were chomping away at fresh green grass just like cows and some of them were almost as big as cows – the Giant Grazing Pigs of Indiana.

Our on-going cold war with roadside dogs turned hot today. We were riding through a charming neighborhood along a winding, narrow Indiana road when a massive brute of a dog charged us. Luckily he was old and faltered after the initial charge. In the next half mile however, four more tag teams of two large dogs each came at us from either side. I was ready for them and had the BB pistol drawn and ready to fire. Like some Hollywood action hero I was firing left, then right, then left again. The BB's found their marks and the dogs quit the chase but I was disappointed that the dogs seemed more perplexed by the hits than pained by them. I was expecting a BB hit to produce a yelp of pain and a dog making for home with his tail between his legs. Their response was more like a "what-was-that?" look of consternation. Still, I'd have to say the pistol did its job as the dogs left us alone after being hit. We discovered a weakness in our ACD (Anti-Canine-Defense) System though. Like some early WWII bombers we were vulnerable to attack from the rear. That's because I can't get a good aim on a dog that comes in from behind and Mary (our tail gunner) isn't interested in handling the pistol. Let's just hope the word doesn't get out.

We crossed paths with another cycle tourist today. Just after crossing a small north-south highway near Monon we stopped to look at our map and I caught a glimpse of a lone rider behind us, heading south on the road we had just crossed. Our view of the highway was shuttered by tall stands of corn so it was a very brief glimpse and the rider had disappeared by the time I thought to hail him. His bike's panniers marked him as one of us. We can't get over how few and far between our fellow bikers are or how common it is for them to travel alone. In fact, every one of the twenty or so cycle tourists we have encountered has been traveling alone. That amazes me. If ever there were a time for companionship it would be on a long bicycle ride. What is it about long distance riders that makes them such loners – men and women? Those single young women we met in Montana were definitely cut from a different cloth than their peers.

And this coming from a guy, who as a young man often motored, biked and backpacked alone so I speak with some authority on this subject. In my case, it wasn't that I didn't want companions but that I was very choosy about who my companions were. I was never a person to hang out with peers just to keep myself from being alone. I think I always thought of friendship in an idealized way and if my companions weren't *good* friends, I had no use for them. When it came to traveling, I didn't want to be bothered to seek someone else out or to have to deal with their problems once we hit the road or trail unless I felt a close bond with them. Pair that attitude with the fact that I rarely made the overtures that are usually necessary to make friends and you have a person who spends a lot of time alone. I took a trip with only my dog Boo as company in my '61 Ford van in the autumn of 1972 after graduating from college. I traveled from Southern California to Maine over many of the very roads we are now following. My purpose was very similar to ours – I just wanted to see the country. I remember telling myself on that trip that I'd like to redo it someday with a hot chick who was crazy-in-love with me and although Mary would scoff at the suggestion that she is "hot" or that she's crazy-in-love with me I think both are true. I wonder if the motivation for traveling alone is the same for these bikers we have met. I'd like to ask some of them but Mary thinks I shouldn't because it's too personal a question for a roadside encounter.

So I said "Geez, Mary, it's not like I'm going to say "So, are you traveling alone because no one could stand to be with you, or what?"

Whereupon she looked at me with a steady gaze that said "Don't make me say it Lief, but that's exactly the kind of thing you'd say." Well, maybe. I am something of a loose cannon at times.

September 21, 2006; Day 34; Mile 2826; Wabash, Indiana to Paulding, Ohio: Autumn is in the air. It must have been in the low forties this morning and some of the trees are starting to lose their leaves. We've seen pumpkins stacked in front of farm houses and bundles of dried corn stalks arranged in harvest displays. The trappings of summer's end are everywhere to be seen. I hope we get to New England in time for the colorful leaves.

The weather forecast for tomorrow is scattered showers and rain over the weekend. So far we have been very lucky as far as the weather. It was rather hot during our first week and we had a few days of headwind in North Dakota and Minnesota but most of the days have been sunny and pleasant. We often hear tales from the locals of other cyclists who came through during the summer heat and we can only shake our heads and wonder why September vacations aren't more popular. We know there aren't many like us because we have only seen a handful of other distance cyclists in the last three weeks and we're on a popular route.

Now, to change the subject to one that some may think rather indelicate but one that I think needs speaking to – butts and their interaction with bicycle seats. If you're contemplating a bicycle ride of more than 50 miles, don't worry about whether your legs are strong enough – get a seat that you can sit on all day without doing yourself damage. It is a far more relevant issue for most people.

Mary is still dealing with saddle soreness issues on a daily basis and we're almost 3000 miles and 34 days into this trip. She tried four different seats, several costing over $100 each before we started our ride and none of them was comfortable for more than an hour at a time. Even now we have to stop several times an hour for what she calls a "butt rubbing party" and she has to stand on her pedals every ten minutes "to increase blood flow." She continues to have abrasions and raw skin from the seat. Each night she applies ointments, the best being one marketed for babies and diaper rash – "Balmex."

Perhaps the best piece of seat technology we have found was a $10 gel seat cover at Wal Mart – not the place one usually thinks of for quality sporting goods.

Along the lines of the old adage "Put a hat on your head to warm your feet" I have found the best way to avoid butt issues is an addition to my handlebar. It's called an Aerobar and it's an extension clamped on my handlebar which allows me to rest my elbows on pads and hold onto hand grips that extend forward of the regular bars. This takes a considerable amount of weight off my butt and thus eases the "load." Consequently, I have had no problem with my seat. Mary is unable to use an Aerobar because my seat is forward of her handlebar and thus is in the way.

Oh, and by the way, we have a new recipient of the Lief Carlsen Award for Best Deal in Motel Accommodations. Tonight we're staying at the "Bittersweet Inn" in Paulding, Ohio and it's a very nice room with kitchenette for $45. Until now the title holder was "LeAnn's Motel" in Poplar, Montana which beat this place for price ($35) but was considerably less elegant. Both are spotlessly clean.

September 22, 2006; Day 35; Mile 2891; Paulding to Bowling Green, Ohio: Rained off and on today but not so hard we couldn't ride on through it. Ohio, at least in the northwestern part we are traveling through, is less agricultural than the areas we've come through so far. By tomorrow we should reach the shore of Lake Erie and farms will give way entirely to residential/industrial.

We stopped at a bicycle store in Defiance which is the first one we have been able to catch during business hours since Sandpoint, Idaho. We were hopeful the store mechanic could help us solve the mystery of the persistent noise our bike is making. The mechanic in Defiance said he was "99% sure" the cause was the bearing retainer ring on the rear crank which he torqued and pronounced "fixed." A mile out of town the bike started groaning and squeaking again. Oh well, the bike still carries us forward each day and has for the last thousand miles. Hopefully it will get us through the next thousand without serious breakdown too.

Passed by some titanic wind turbines outside of Tontogany. It's hard to describe how impressive these behemoths are as you approach them from afar and finally stand at their bases. They are like skyscrapers amid the corn fields with their blades turning in perfect synchronicity which lends them just a hint of other-worldliness. To my surprise, I found the whole experience quite emotional. They are, in a word, awesome. To think there are those who oppose their installation on esthetic or environmental grounds. I don't understand such people.

We had a little surprise waiting for us when we arrived at our destination this afternoon, Bowling Green. This is the weekend of a big football game against Kent State and the town is hopping. I always thought BGSU was in Kentucky! Rooms at the Best Western are going for $120 so we're slapping cockroaches on the wall and slumming it at an unusually cheesy Day's Inn. Rain forecasted for tonight and tomorrow.

September 23, 2006; Day 36; Mile 2971; Bowling Green to Vermilion, Ohio: Tonight we sleep on the southern shore of Lake Erie; tomorrow we make our way through the metropolis of Cleveland and its suburbs. The prophesized rain never materialized today though heavy clouds filled the sky in every direction all through the day and road surfaces were wet wherever we went. Who was that character in Al Capp's Li'l Abner who always had a rain cloud follow him wherever he went? We were his negative image today. Evidence of rain was all around us but never on us. It appears we have dodged a bullet once again as the weather is forecasted to be fair.

Today's ride was pleasant enough though heavy with humidity as we passed through decidedly flat country with a jaunty tailwind. The small city of Fremont was as splendid an assemblage of architecture and landscaping as I have ever seen. Magnificent boulevards lined with stately trees and imposing mansions from early in the last century and all of it kept in fine repair. A first-rate, paved bicycle trail began at the city center and went all nine miles to the town of Clyde. If only such a trail crossed the entire country what a joy bicycling would be.

Not for the first time on our journey we encountered a detour across our path today. It is no small matter for a bicycle to travel miles out of its way and so, with a "damn-the-torpedoes, full-speed-ahead!" attitude, we continued on our prescribed course. The reason for the detour turned out to be a small bridge under construction across a drainage canal. It being a Saturday, no workmen were present at the site. We dismounted and walked our bicycle down into the cavernous ditch and with considerable effort pushed it up the steep bank on the other side. I was quite surprised that Mary thought the whole endeavor great fun as she is usually loath to break any of society's rules and ignoring a detour must certainly qualify as rule breaking. Once on the other side we resumed our progress toward the next town without delay and considered our unauthorized crossing a satisfying, if somewhat naughty, success.

With our long bicycle and our baggage we're obviously up to something out of the ordinary and we answer a number of questions from the curious every day wherever we are. Once they know where we're going and where we came from, one of the questions/comments we often hear is "How do you tolerate each other's company day after day? If my husband and I were stuck on a bicycle together we'd be at each other's throats." About this time Mary and I look at each other and shrug our shoulders. We really don't know why we get along or don't and we certainly have been known to annoy each other on occasion. I'd say in general we enjoy each other's company but each of us has definite triggers that set us off. I get irritated when I set my mind to do something and stuff gets in the way – like when I expect to ride 90 miles and Mary dawdles over her coffee or wants to stop and rest all the time. Mary's trigger is similar to that of a small child who hasn't had his bottle or nap. She gets cranky in the afternoon when she's tired and/or hungry.

But she's unpredictable. Some days, like today, she gets to laughing about 2 or 3 PM over practically nothing. It could be something I say or even the way I move or something that happened several days earlier. She'll get to thinking about it and start laughing so hard that it feels like she's going to fall off the bike. And don't think she's having a wonderful time back there doing all that laughing. She's got some weird neurological connection between laughter and leg cramps so that her laughter is often punctuated by howls of pain. Luckily, a hot shower and a meal will almost always restore her sanity so that most days end well.

September 24, 2006; Day 37; Mile 3087; Vermilion to Ashtabula, Ohio: After riding through 3000 miles of farm land we spent the day riding through 60 miles of city today – Cleveland, to be specific and for the first half of the day I enjoyed it. Coming from Vermilion on the west side of the city we followed the road which runs along the lake. Houses line the shore for 40 miles on either side of the city. It was interesting to watch them grow larger and more imposing as we neared Cleveland itself. By the time we were within a few miles of downtown the houses were Vanderbilt-class mansions.

Cleveland Skyline

Downtown Cleveland was abuzz today with football fever. The Browns' stadium is there on the waterfront and a home game was scheduled. Tailgate parties filled the parking lot and we found ourselves riding through throngs of excited fans who hurried toward the stadium. A brisk wind blew cotton-ball clouds across the blue sky over Lake Erie and pushed waves against the seawall. Country bumpkins that we are, we passed through this world of skyscrapers and professional football with our eyes wide and our mouths agog. This was a slice of the world one sees on TV and we were in the thick of it. It seemed like a great day for football.

Leaving downtown toward the eastern suburbs was a different story. We passed through neighborhoods of public housing. Urban decay and its attendant problems of bad road surfaces, shuttered businesses, derelicts hanging out on the streets, and broken glass on the road extended for at least ten miles from downtown. We stopped at a McDonalds for some lunch. I waited outside. Mary went in and didn't return for 15 minutes. She finally came out disgusted and angry. She said she had ordered and paid for a meal but the workers were so disorganized they never got around to serving her. She gave up and came out with nothing.

For my part, I spent the time Mary was in McDonald's listening to the ramblings of a fat, bearded, Yugoslavian immigrant who, by his own reckoning, had earned millions of dollars, had sex with scores of beautiful and exotic women (he produced well-worn photos from his wallet as "proof"), and repeatedly been screwed over by his ungrateful children. As to why he would choose to share all this with me, a stranger sitting on the curb outside McDonald's, well, that's what I was wondering too.

After spending our afternoon on the wrong side of town we were ready to return to farm land. I find it hard to believe anyone would live in a place like that by choice. To judge by what we saw, I'd say that whole side of the city is dysfunctional.

By late in the day we had escaped the madness that is East Cleveland and found refuge in the rural countryside along Lake Erie – this despite a sky that had turned dark and a lake that was stormy. Waves worthy of an ocean slapped against the shore. We checked into renting a cabin on the lake shore from which to watch the storm but it was too late in the season and most had closed down for the year. Geneva-On-The-Lake was our destination because it had an appealing name on the map but in reality it was pretty trashy so we moved on to Ashtabula which isn't much better but we got a room anyway because it was beginning to rain and getting dark.

September 25, 2006; Day 38; Mile 3177; Ashtabula, Ohio to Dunkirk, NY: This morning we started in Ohio, crossed Pennsylvania (the NW corner) and advanced thirty miles into New York. It was a great day of riding – Pennsylvania and New York proved to be gracious hosts by providing us with nice road surfaces with wide shoulders. It was a welcome relief after Ohio's sorry pavement. The weather god is also still cooperating by providing tail wind and sunshine and a perfect 65 degrees. The final dash of perfection was the smell of grape jelly in the air most of the day as we rode through thousands of acres of concord grapes that are fully ripe and ready to be picked (I stopped and sampled a few, just to be sure).

Taking a break on the shore of Lake Erie
Our internal clocks seem to have caught up to the mechanical ones now. While in Indiana we were surprised to find ourselves subjected to Eastern Time so far west. The world seemed a little out of sync. I believe the technical word for this is "bike lag" and one would think it should be milder than its more recognized cousin, jet lag, as we are only progressing eastward at a rate of 12 to 15 mph, but it seemed to do a number on us all the same.

The economic decline I wrote of earlier in the agricultural areas of Montana and North Dakota is more widespread than I realized. Almost every town we have stopped in during our crossing of the country has a shrunken commercial district and surplus housing that is badly in need of repair. Dunkirk, NY, to judge by the buildings in town, was once a thriving mid-sized city. It looks like a ghost town now. In Ohio and New York the economies appear to have been industrial-based and I guess those industries are no longer competitive. The last town I remember as a vital, growing one was clear back in

Whitefish, Montana. It is as if Adventure Cycling Association, the people who put together our guide map, had gone out of their way to find declining economies. I don't think that is the case but we have been treated to a front-row seat of the changing economy. The likely explanation is that dead towns don't have much traffic and automobile traffic is what bicyclists want to avoid, hence, this route.

September 26, 2006; Day 39; Mile 3177; Dunkirk, NY to Niagara Falls, Canada: What the heck, we thought; it's a once-in-a-lifetime type of thing. So we rented a room with a view of Niagara Falls in the fanciest hotel we could find – the Fallsview Casino Resort. Such luxury, of course, doesn't come cheap and it would have cost us a lot more if the nice young fellow named Bruno at the check-in counter hadn't responded to Mary's request for a "bicycle rider's discount" (whatever that is) and knocked $82 off our rate. We tried to atone for our guilt over spending so much on a hotel room later in the evening when we shared a single Subway sandwich for our dinner (weak-willed beings that we are, we relented within the hour and supplemented our

Room With a View

meager meal with a slice of pizza.) I must say, however, it's a very nice room and the view of the falls is indeed spectacular. I think we're cut out to live this way. I rather like it. If only nice things didn't cost so much!

Getting here from Dunkirk involved riding through Buffalo, NY which was like visiting the set of HBO's hit show *The Sopranos*. We came through a sort of Little Italy section of town which had a lot of fast food places where you normally can find public restrooms only these didn't have restrooms. I don't know if Italians don't have to pee as often as other people or what but we couldn't find a place to go so we stopped at a cathedral and, sure enough, found what we needed in the basement. While Mary was "taking her turn" I was sitting on a low wall outside looking at our map. Several people stopped to talk to me. They asked the usual questions about our bike but then went on and on about a certain Father Baker who was the priest who raised the money to build the cathedral with the much-needed bathroom in its basement. They urged me to touch his casket which is inside the cathedral as it would assure me of good fortune and they told me of all the people Father Baker had helped while he was alive.

When we walked across the street to have lunch in a café, the couple at the table next to us volunteered more tales about the great Father Baker. The husband lifted the sleeve of his shirt to show us a tattoo of Father Baker on his arm. It was Father Baker this and Father Baker that wherever we went. Father Baker must have been one hell of a guy. This whole neighborhood seems obsessed with him.

About *The Sopranos* – in addition to all the people around the cathedral and the café talking with the accents of Soprano characters they looked like them! One woman

who was curious about our bike looked just like Ralphy's wife and had the identical, cigarette-induced husky voice and accent. Another woman at the café had the same bouffant hairdo as the fat wife of the New York mob boss, Johnny Sack. When we paid our tab the waitress actually said "<u>Yous</u> ride carefully and have a nice day." Wow! Real New York Italians.

Despite a detailed map we had trouble finding our way through Buffalo to the border crossing into Canada. We spent a lot of time asking whomever was handy for directions and trying to line up the map with the city sights in front of us. When we finally stepped up for our Customs inspection I was a little nervous about the reception my pistol would get. I figured the best tactic was to tell him right up front about it. I did my best to prepare him but when I pulled it out of the pannier he still stepped back a little in surprise like he thought I was going to pump him full of lead. I guess it's a pretty good facsimile of an automatic 9 mm or something. I explained about the dogs and wouldn't have been surprised if he denied us permission to bring it in to Canada but all he said was "Don't shoot any Canadian dogs please."

We followed the Niagara River from its source in Lake Erie (which is also the border crossing) north about 15 miles to Niagara Falls on the Canadian side of the river following a very nice bike path that fronts a residential neighborhood. For some reason I'm profoundly disoriented in this area and cannot mesh what I see with what the map shows. No matter how many times I tell myself that this river is running north into Lake Ontario my brain goes right back to assuming it is running south. Now I know how Mary must feel because she's always having trouble telling north from south.

There are some things that cameras can improve over real life (like aging movie stars' faces) and some things to which they can't do justice. Niagara Falls most emphatically belongs to the latter category. What a thrill to stand just to one side of Horseshoe Falls and feel the power of that falling water! I tried a few camera angles but realized my efforts were in vain so I wound up not taking any pictures of the falls themselves. It would have been disrespectful to cheapen their grandeur by taking photos that portray them as anything less than magnificent.

We're sitting at the window of our hotel room just now enjoying the view of the city lights and the colored spotlights trained on the falls and I'm thinking that I'm going to awaken in the night and realize in my sleepy brain that I'm in a luxury hotel at Niagara Falls and it's going to seem so weird to me. I realize that what I'm trying to say is probably not entirely clear to anyone, including me, so, for the benefit of all of us let me attempt an explanation: Everyday life, a humdrum existence if you will, may lack the element of excitement but it has the advantage of imparting the illusion of security by virtue of its constancy, i.e., if my life doesn't change much, it may not get much better but at least it won't get much worse – a feeling more succinctly expressed in the adage "Prefer the devil you know to the devil you don't know." Enjoyable as it may be, staying in luxury hotels and crossing the country on a bicycle is not my usual lot in life. The novelty of it, at this moment, has the effect of suggesting the possibility of significant change (good or bad) in the rest of my life which, on the whole, is not a bad life so I'm not entirely comfortable with the notion of change to the status quo. Now, logically, I know that it does not follow that, because I'm staying in a luxury hotel tonight, tomorrow will be different than it otherwise would. But the idea that we can magically alter the course of future events – through incantations, voodoo dolls, appeals to a higher power, lucky charms, etc. – seems to be hard wired into the human brain and I am not exempt from such thoughts. Thus I find myself amidst the splendor of these accommodations laboring to flush from my thoughts the absurd notion that there is any connection between where I sleep tonight and my serenity two years down the road. I suppose it's thoughts like this that have New York Italians scurrying to touch Father Baker's casket for reassurance.

"On the Erie Canal"

September 27, 2006; Day 40; Mile 3267; Niagara Falls to Rochester, NY: Late start this morning. We wanted to soak up a little more luxury from our wonderful hotel room before leaving. The dawn (a pink horizon under purple clouds over the city) was exquisite from our room on the 27th floor overlooking Niagara Falls. We took one last look around at the tasteful furnishings and delightful color scheme before leaving. This luxury kinda' grows on you.

A perfect example is what happened tonight. We tried a few two-star motels in Rochester and found the prices high so we located a Motel 6 and had actually checked in. When we opened the door to our room it looked as if someone had rebuilt an engine on the carpet. I mean, there were grimy smudges everywhere and an unidentified odor in the air. We checked back out and wound up paying $100 for what I consider a $50 room at another motel. Yep, we're spoiled.

The other day I had mentioned that we have ridden past a lot of snakes since crossing the Mississippi. Mary said that she hadn't seen any so I said I would point out the next one I saw. Well, we passed a little one today which Mary failed to see so I turned the bike around and rode back to show her the snake. There was no traffic on the road and we were going very slow as we turned – too slow as it turned out. We started going over and, knowing that Mary requires a little time to extricate herself from the bike because her shoes clip to her pedals, I tried valiantly to stop our fall – to no avail. Whomp! We hit the asphalt like a felled tree hits the forest floor. I wound up on my back and Mary lay on her side with her feet still attached to her pedals. I stood up and checked to see that all my parts were still there. My left hand was missing a little skin and my middle finger felt a little funny but otherwise I seemed OK. After unclipping her shoes from her pedals Mary slowly rose and did a quick inventory – no lasting damage.

This little incident is a great example of why I refuse to wear clip-in bicycle shoes even though "everybody's" doing it. Had Mary been wearing "normal" shoes like me, she could have simply put one leg out to stop our fall and that would have been the end of it. But the vogue among our bicycle-riding friends these days is to imitate the riding attire of professional cyclists as much as possible and that includes expensive shoes that clip into special pedals. Never mind that the advantage this combination confers on the rider is only noticeable at the highest levels of competition – a category that hardly describes us. If that's what everybody else is doing, Mary's going to go along with the crowd even if it means following her bicycle over a cliff or falling over like a bowling pin when she approaches a stop sign. Not Lief. No sireee. I'll keep my rubber-soled running shoes and $5, flat pedals thank you.

We had a great day of riding though. The historic Erie Canal, which was built in the early nineteenth century and revolutionized transportation in the newly independent USA, still exists and even though it no longer transports lumber, coal, and hay from New York's interior to the City it has found new life as a bicycle trail. The tow path where "a mule named Sal" once pulled barges, is now a great bike path: perfectly flat, smooth surfaced, scenic. If you like riding a bike but don't like hills or cars you should consider riding the Erie Canal. New York has a 500-mile network of bike paths that follow old canals. I don't know about the rest of the year but in late September we practically had the 90 miles of bike trail on our route to ourselves.

Still having great weather. Sunny with a warm breeze that felt like it blew in from Cancun, Mexico. I think our luck is about to run out, though. They're calling for rain and cold tomorrow or the next day.

September 28, 2006; Day 41; Mile 3327; Rochester to Sodus Point, NY: Our charmed relationship with weather has ended and we have at last earned our stripes as true touring cyclists by slogging through a day of hard rain. Even though we knew the rain was coming it was intimidating to a couple of fair-weather riders such as we to finally experience a deluge. Our rain jackets kept us more or less dry but extremities were exposed and soaked. Fortunately the rain was rather warm. Should we meet a cold storm I expect we will have no choice but to hunker down in a hotel until it ends as we have little in the way of warm clothing.

We went on a pilgrimage of sorts this morning. Mary read in some guide notes that a town just off the canal, Macedon, is the home of Terry Precision Cycling. Terry is a company with a respected reputation among cycling women because it supposedly builds bicycles and accessories catering to women's "special needs." As my use of quotation marks suggest, I have my doubts that the company caters to anything more substantial than women's desire to be catered to. Nonetheless, Mary counts herself among the faithful and so it was that we set off looking to find Terry headquarters in Macedon like gravely ill supplicants at a religious shrine, hoping that a drink of blessed water (or, in this case engineering) would provide the cure for Mary's suffering. Her particular ailment is the saddle soreness that I have mentioned before – saddle soreness of a feminine nature. Mary has tried countless bicycle seats over the years in an attempt to find one that solves her problem – all to no avail. She figured that if anyone could solve this problem (and she believes it is widespread but rarely talked about among women) it would be the Terry company. Despite my skepticism that Terry would have any answers, I encouraged Mary to make the detour into Macedon because I have tremendous sympathy for her. Having witnessed how every day of this trip she has had to contend with female problems in addition to the usual travails that all cyclists endure, had me hoping for a miracle too.

As it turned out, no one in Macedon that we could find had ever heard of Terry Precision Cycling. We found this surprising as Macedon isn't that big and we figured a company of any size would stand out in a small town. After consulting a phone book we finally got an address which placed it on a road out of town. The rain had started with our arrival in Macedon but we had an important mission and a little rain wasn't going to stop us. Mary intended to present her case to the Terry design engineers and see if they already had or could build a seat for women that would accommodate their special anatomical needs. Well, like I said, a little rain couldn't stop us but the downpour we encountered a mile or two out of Macedon was definitely dampening Mary's enthusiasm. We continued on for several more soaking-wet miles and looked left and right and couldn't find anything that looked like the Terry company. We were practically drowning in rainwater when Mary called it quits. If the company wasn't there, it wasn't there. What could she do?

Defeated by the elusive location of the Terry company and thoroughly soaked, we rode back through Macedon and made our way to the next town which is Palmyra. By the time we got there Mary was feeling pretty low. She said she wanted to find a place to get out of the rain and quit for the day despite having only made thirty miles of actual progress. I was glad that we hadn't confronted such travails early in our trip because I think Mary would have given up and gone home if there had been an easy out at that point. It amazes me sometimes how she allows little setbacks to bring her down. Fortunately, there was no easy way out. Our map listed three bed & breakfasts which we located but they each looked rather shabby so she agreed to press on. Once we got to pedaling in earnest our exertions warmed us to the point where it really wasn't that bad (at least I didn't think so). Mary is a little more inclined than I to see the unpleasant side of physical hardship and she made it clear she didn't enjoy the second half of our ride. She did her part though and we made it sixty miles to lodging in this little town on Lake Ontario.

Riding in heavy rain is a whole different experience than fair-weather riding and I'm not just talking about getting wet. I think the psychological contrast is even greater than the physical contrast. When the weather is nice, I feel like one of the privileged few – a lucky guy – when I'm on a bike. I look at the people in cars and think how much better I have it than they do. Don't they know how much fun it is to ride a bike? But when the sky is dark and rain drips into every crevice of my clothing and the passing cars splash us, the table turns. I know that the people in each of those cars are warm and dry while I'm cold and wet and I start feeling like an outsider, a pariah. I feel a lot like I imagine a homeless guy must feel on a cold night when he walks down a residential street and sees families all warm and together at the dinner table – left out. If I had been doing this trip solo I think I would have felt as crummy as Mary in today's rain. But knowing she and I are in this together makes a big difference to me.

When we got to Sodus Point we were literally dripping puddles of rainwater on the hardwood floor of the B&B as we stood in the foyer talking to the owner. We took our stuff up to our room, put on our dry clothes and walked to town where we had supper in a tavern decorated with pirate paraphernalia. We ate our cheeseburgers and fries in that darkened tavern as the jukebox blared and the rain came down outside and I kept looking at Mary and thinking how pretty she is and how lucky I am that she's my wife and companion even if she does get easily discouraged and go negative on me sometimes.

September 29, 2006; Day 42; Mile 3410; Sodus Point to Pulaski, NY: When I worked for the Forest Service we dug fire line with a tool whose business end was an axe on one side and a hoe on the other called a Pulaski (pronounced "puh LAS key"). Today, when I spoke of their town as if it were my trusty axe/hoe of old, the locals in Pulaski, NY politely corrected my pronunciation on several occasions to "puh LAS ki" (ki = k+eye.) Pulaski, we discovered to our dismay, is a small town of 2,000 inhabitants near eastern Lake Ontario that hosts about 10,000 frenzied salmon fishermen (in the words of one disparaging local, "fish heads") on this weekend each year. We arrived in town about 7 PM, tired from our day's ride and expecting to get a room at the local Super 8 Motel.

The desk clerk merely laughed at our request. She told us we had to have reservations at least a year in advance for salmon week.

So there we were, the sun going down, our camping gear sent back to Chelan, straddling our bicycle wondering if we were going to have to commit some petty crime to get a bed in the local jail for the night. What to do? Our trusty guide map listed a Brenda's Motel five miles out of town on a country road. To our great relief, a phone call ascertained that Brenda did have a "room" (which turned out to be a trailer decorated with four frenzied fishermen in mind and not my persnickety wife.) After careful consideration of the options open to us, we ageed to pay Brenda her four-star-hotel-asking price and were glad to do it. But first we had to get there. By this time it was dark and we had five miles of unlit road to traverse with a steady stream of speeding cars. Mary was freaking out that we were going to be run over but I assured her that we show up better at night in our orange construction vests with reflective striping than we do in the day. My primary concern was not the passing cars but seeing the road by the light of our pitifully weak headlamp. After a knuckle-whitening five-mile ride we arrived at Brenda's in two pieces (one each).

After yesterday's ride in the rain we started out under a dark sky this morning with considerable trepidation. The weather was cool to be sure but afternoon sunshine cast a whole different light on things. Isn't it amazing how much nicer the world looks in sunlight – especially autumn leaves? Which reminds me of something I have been meaning to bring up for some time – the foliage. Until today we hadn't seen any color other than green with the occasional exception of a red sumac and I was somewhat concerned that New England's vaunted leaves of autumn might be a bust this year. Since we'll be entering the

Adirondack Mountains tomorrow and Vermont after that it is about time for some color. Well, we're starting to see some and we're told it is more pronounced to the east. Just in time!

We ran over an acorn this morning and in addition to making a loud cracking/exploding sound it gave us a flat. While patching the inner tube I noticed that our front tire was worn through in several places so we made a point of stopping at the next town with a bike shop. He didn't have our size tire but called ahead to another town (Oswego) and found some for us. Oswego is off route about ten miles but it could have been our only opportunity to get tires for many miles so we rode there and the guys at Murdoch's Bike shop spent several hours taking our bike apart and greasing everything in an attempt to find the mystery squeak that has been plaguing us for much of the trip. Three other bike mechanics have attempted to solve the mystery and failed. The Murdoch guys really went to great lengths to check everything they could think of that might be the squeak's source and then amazed us by refusing any pay for their work! They said they never charge for their labor when they work on touring cyclists' bikes. You'd think we were war heroes of something the way people treat us. We're not complaining.

The mystery squeak? Still squeaking and still a mystery.

September 30, 2006; Day 43; Miles 3483; Pulaski to Old Forge, NY: The big story of the day is spelled r-e-l-i-e-f. We had been riding on the usual quiet back roads all day and they were just that – quiet. When we turned onto SR 28, a secondary highway and nine miles short of our destination, we encountered nearly bumper-to-bumper traffic and our hearts sank. Had we again been cursed to arrive in a town at just the time when some special event had pre-empted all the motel rooms? We speculated that the busy traffic was city folk out for the weekend to see the fall foliage. Once more faced with the prospect of being shelter-less for the night, we brainstormed different ways to throw ourselves on the mercy of some kind-hearted organization or individual as we rode the final miles into Old Forge. The little town was indeed crowded with leaf watchers but we found a motel room and our hearts are glad.

Steady rain is predicted for tomorrow and we're toying with the idea of spending a day in Old Forge. I've been reading David McCullough's new book *1776* about the American Revolution and I wouldn't mind finishing it. It's very good. The strange thing about reading that book is that as much as I admire George Washington and think America is the best thing that ever happened to civilization, I think I would have been a loyalist (to King George) had I lived during those times. Revolutions as a whole are such messy affairs and usually don't turn out so well as ours. I doubt I would have had much faith in the rebels (American patriots). When the security of everyday life is tenuous, when chaos reigns supreme, and a revolution is certainly such a time, the self-interest that is the driving engine of our actions will assert itself. Forbearance and generosity are luxuries made possible when artificial rules are imposed from without by authority vested in a benign government. The peace and prosperity of America are exceptional when seen against the sweep of history. To walk away from the tranquility provided by an established government in a search for a pie-in-the-sky, better society seems like a wager with very poor odds.

Does that paragraph of pessimism stand in sharp contrast with my observation that we have repeatedly benefited from the kindness of strangers on this trip? Maybe. But I think selfishness and generosity reside in all of us. Under the right conditions generosity comes to the fore. Under the wrong conditions, selfishness takes over. That duality is precisely why I would have remained loyal to the king – he provided the best opportunity for our better natures to shine forth. We are *so* fortunate as Americans that we have been blessed with wise leaders like George Washington and Abraham Lincoln when our stability was in peril.

October 1, 2006; Day 44; Mile 3483; Old Forge, NY: That's no typo; we're still at mile 3483 because we haven't gone anywhere today. This makes only our second day of rest on the entire trip and we had good reason – steady rain forecasted. In actuality, the rain has been merely sporadic but Old Forge is a lively little tourist town and not a bad place to spend a lazy day so we've enjoyed it.

The trees are colorful here and the air has the requisite crispness for a proper fall day. We are entering our last week of riding and already thinking back over where we've been and what we've done in a bit of premature nostalgia. This business of riding a bicycle all day has become a way of life and we're quite used to it. In fact, today feels somewhat unnatural because we aren't riding.

The topography has been notably flat since the Mississippi River and we are just now getting back into hill country. The locals have been telling us horror stories about all the steep grades ahead going through the Adirondacks and Vermont/New Hampshire. In the face of such talk I just remind Mary of Logan Pass in the Rockies and how we did 70 miles and climbed to 7000 feet all in the same day. If we could do that we can do anything these puny eastern mountains can throw our way. Mary likes to counter with the example of the relentless succession of small hills near New Town, ND which almost kicked our butts.

This subject of hills reminds me of an encounter I had earlier in the trip where a woman in a restaurant was talking to me about the hills up the road and then added, as an afterthought, "Of course you'll get to coast down the other side so they're really no harder than pedaling on flat ground." I thought to myself "I'd like to see you pedal your [considerable derriere] up one side of those hills and down the other." What actually came out of my mouth was a rather impassioned physics lecture explaining that one uphill and one downhill do not cancel each other. I emphatically pointed out to her that if we lived on a planet without an atmosphere she might have a point but that much of the energy gained by climbing a hill on planet Earth is lost pushing air out of the way when you go down the other side. When I had finished I noticed she looked somewhat taken aback by my verbal onslaught and hurried over to her husband without saying another word. Her hasty retreat got me thinking I had been a bit hard on the poor woman who, after all, was only making polite conversation and probably didn't give a hoot about the physics of bicycle riding. I might even have walked over and apologized had her husband not shepherded her out the door about this time with a worried backward glance at me.

I think I learned something about Mary today. We were eating some breakfast in a little restaurant in Old Forge and Mary was talking to the waitress about our bicycle ride as she has with countless people along the way. I wasn't saying much – I never do when this subject comes up because it kind of bores me. The ride certainly doesn't bore me but talking about it does because after telling the story a few times the process has become stale.

Mary sharing our story with the curious.

That doesn't seem to be an issue for Mary. She continues to be amazed that she has been able to pull off this ride – and here's the thing I realized at breakfast today: *she sees herself as a kind of ambassador to the sedentary*. She wants to spread the gospel that ordinary people can do extraordinary things and she believes she is the proof of that. She would be the perfect publicity agent if we had need for one. She lights up on these occasions; she's positively delighted. She revels in the role of celebrity. Too bad she's not a movie star; she'd be great with her fans.

October 2, 2006; Day 45; Mile 3567; Old Forge to North Hudson, NY: We have crossed the Hudson and New England beckons. Our journey through the Adirondacks showed those mountains to be little more than foothills and scarcely a challenge. If only the Appalachians are as meager we will reach the Atlantic considerably ahead of schedule. Still, I won't count those un-hatched chicks quite yet.

The day was disappointingly overcast. The few sun breaks we had cast a heartening spotlight on the variously colored trees, however, and I hope we get at least one full day of sunshine before we leave Vermont and New Hampshire. Thursday (this is a Monday) is the first day forecasted to be clear. At our current rate of progress we will be leaving New Hampshire by then and may miss the big show. We might have to tarry another day to be in the right place at the right time.

Expecting an arduous ride, we made an early start from Old Forge this morning. Dark clouds filled the sky and a light

mist seemed to contradict the forecast of "partly cloudy." Still, the trees of the surrounding hills were beautiful with their red, orange, yellow and green leaves. The first half hour of riding in the morning is always my favorite time. The bike seems to glide so effortlessly when we start. I suppose that's because we are refreshed from our night's rest but it seems such a perfect machine at the start of the day that I delight in its motion. When the days were hot, the morning coolness was another bonus but now it is the quiet of a still-waking town through which we glide like ghosts that makes this time special.

The first ten miles usually go quickly and today was no exception. We would be following a chain of lakes (known, incidentally, as the Fulton Chain Lakes) much of the day. Their shores in many places are massive rock cliffs interspersed with small sandy beaches that make them perfect locations for summer cottages – a fact well-off New Yorkers have taken full advantage of by building cabins of all descriptions wherever possible. Curious what it would cost to join the fortunate few who own a piece of these lakes, we stopped at a real estate office at Raquette Lake and asked (a two-bedroom, on the lake, from $500,000 to $1,000,000.)

When the day is going well, we have usually covered around 40 miles by noon. Today was going very well as we reached that milestone by 11:00. Mary likes her coffee, usually several times a day, so we stopped at Long Lake, one of the few little towns on today's route, for a cup. In my pre-bicycle-tourist life, I rarely drank the stuff but it's no fun sitting idly by while Mary sips coffee for twenty minutes so I have become a convert. Actually, I still detest straight coffee but Mary has taught me how to cover the bitterness with heavy spikes of cream and sugar.

Early afternoons can be discouraging. Just as the first ten miles seem to go quickly, the middle twenty seem to take forever. Like so much of bicycling, the answer lies in perception. The newness of the day is gone by then and saddle soreness has begun to take its toll. Forty or fifty miles remain and at that time of the day that seems like a lot. We usually compensate by taking more breaks or a long lunch to chop this segment into manageable pieces. Today, we stopped at a little bar/grill at Newcomb for a cheeseburger and fries. The place was more of a bar than a grill and the meal gave us both indigestion but it did provide the much-needed break and fueled us up for the afternoon ride. Stopping for meals is also where we usually get a chance to mingle with the locals and get tips on the route ahead or, if we're lucky, some local gossip. Today we got to listen to three broken-down barflies talk about the guns and cars they owned when they were kids. Yawn.

The tips we picked up from the bartender and the trio of barflies turned out to be utterly wrong. The one old guy told us the route to North Hudson was mostly downhill (it had the most difficult climb of the day) and the bartender assured us that we "shouldn't worry about finding a hotel in North Hudson." I don't know what time warp the bar's patrons and tender were living in but in the present-era, the North Hudson we came upon is a ghost town with four empty motels and another colossal abandoned structure, probably a convention center or church. Tall grass grows everywhere in the extensively cracked asphalt parking lots and the town in general has the look of a settlement suddenly abandoned to the bubonic plague or nuclear war. The highway too is in a sad state of repair. Each of its concrete sections is separated from the adjoining ones by tire-destroying gaps of several inches. A dilapidated Jellystone Park Campground still clings to life on the outskirts of town. The paint is faded and peeling from the plywood signs of Yogi Bear and friends who smile and wave to non-existent passersby from the overgrown sides of the highway but, alas, we no longer have camping gear so we pass Yogi by and continue our search for that elusive motel. We find it, at last, ten miles past North Hudson, set serenely against a backdrop of enormous, golden-leafed trees, one car in its parking area and hosted by a perfectly normal lady with a cheery disposition who escorts us to our room as if life went on as usual and the town to the north had not been recently decimated by disease and catastrophe of the worst sort.

October 3, 2006; Day 46; Mile 3652; North Hudson, NY to Bethel, Vermont: The route we're following from New York into Vermont dead ended at Lake Champlain – just stops at the water's edge. Depending on when you arrive, you might have to wait a while but eventually a little 3-car ferry which is guided across the lake by a cable putts up to the truncated highway to take you to Vermont. Cute as can be, it putt putts back across the lake and drops you off where a Vermont farmer's field meets Lake Champlain.

Rain ahead at Vermont summit

This inconspicuous, nearly undeveloped farm land is the place the French chose to build what was, for its day (the early 18th century), a very impressive military base – Fort Ticonderoga. In all of the vastness of North America's interior they chose this place to build a high-tech stone fort with sixty cannon mounted on pointed battlements overlooking the lake. The fort still stands today in excellent repair on the New York side of the lake about half a mile from the little ferry we rode to Vermont. We rode in to take a look at the fort but they wanted $22 each for a walk-through. Mary has no interest whatsoever in historical stuff so she said to count her out and call me cheap but $22 sounded too steep to me so we just kept right on going.

Coincidentally, the book I just finished while we cooled our heels in Old Forge, *1776* by John McCullough, talks about how a young colonel in Washington's army, Henry Knox, astonished everybody by successfully marching a small contingent of Continental soldiers overland from Boston to Ticonderoga and dragging all the cannon back to force the British army and navy to abandon Boston to Washington's forces. When Mary balked at doing an 85-miler today over those same mountains I told her if Knox could do it dragging cannon through the snow, we surely could follow a highway on a bicycle. I think I made my point because there were no more complaints.

The climb out of Middlebury was steep (12% in places) and a hard rain started to fall at the summit of Middlebury Gap but with inspirational thoughts of Henry Knox in our heads we made it to Bethel and this old B&B.

On the ferry we heard about a young couple that had crossed earlier this morning riding bicycles from Washington to Maine (just like us!). Fellow touring cyclists have been so rare on this trip that we responded to this disclosure with a series of penetrating questions worthy of FBI agents: what were their ages? One bike or two? Did they say where they were stopping tonight? We were intensely curious to meet these two fellow travelers.

Steep Vermont Roads

When we walked to town this evening from our B&B to get some pizza we saw two cyclists pass under the train viaduct in the light of a street lamp and round the corner into a darkened street. They were obviously touring cyclists because they were towing Bobs (trailers). I told Mary I thought they might be the mysterious couple we'd heard about earlier in the day. At the pizza parlor I overheard the words "Washington to Maine" in a conversation between the establishment's owner and another customer which struck a chord in my brain since we use those very words to describe our journey to others. I asked him if he was talking about some cyclists and he confirmed that the couple had eaten pizza there just before we arrived (that must have been them we saw earlier!) He said they were camping in the park nearby. We tried to find them because they would be the only people we have met on the entire journey who are traveling the same route in the same direction as we. But alas, it was dark when we left the pizza parlor and we couldn't find the park on the unlit street so we gave up and walked back to the B&B. Perhaps we'll see them in the morning or another day as our itineraries are apparently the same. I hope they don't become another "road legend." There have been several of these – other bicyclists that people tell us about but whom we never meet. Most famous was the family of four from Syracuse, NY who drove out west in an old car which they sold and then started back east on a bicycle built for four. They were a father, mother and two teenagers on one bicycle. Several people in Idaho and Montana told us about them. Funny thing was, every time we heard about them they were either hitching rides or hiring someone to drive them. They always had some reason why they couldn't ride the big bicycle – either it was too hot or the road was too steep. We never heard of them again after Montana so we don't know what happened to them.

This B&B has sullied the reputation of all B&B's for us. It's a real dump, everything is shabby. The corker was when I walked by the living room and saw dog turds on the carpet. At least I think they were dog turds. They were certainly turds. I shudder to think of the alternative explanation.

October 4, 2006; Day 47; Mile 3729; Bethel, Vermont to Woodstock, NH: We located the phantom bike riders this morning. The park they were camping in was just a little farther down the darkened road than we were willing to walk last night. We rode in there this morning as we were leaving town and they were just getting up. They are a young couple from San Diego who have been on the road since June 10. They are on the same course as we but taking smaller steps of about 40 miles/day so we'll probably not see them again. We had a lot to talk about because of our shared experiences. As we were standing at their campsite talking to them I felt a strong sense of admiration for them because they're still camping while we have wimped out by taking the motel route. It's like we've sold our souls for comfort in a way. We have strayed from the righteous path. I know that sounds overstated by that's the way I feel. I guess I see travel as a sort of continuum. At one extreme would be these kids. They're tough and they don't mind a little discomfort. They aren't intimidated by the uncertainties of weather and accommodations and what lies ahead. At the other extreme would be all those tourists you see at places like Niagara Falls who take a taxi the three blocks from their hotels to the Falls because they're too lazy to walk that far. More often than not they're soft and fat and carrying ice cream cones because food is the only pleasure left to them since they've allowed their bodies to fall into such disrepair. I shudder to think I slid a little closer toward the fat tourist end of the continuum when I sent our camping gear back to Chelan. Fearless kids from San Diego, I salute you!

We spent the day on a roller coaster ride through the hills of Vermont and New Hampshire while heavy cloud cover muted the colors we so look forward to seeing. We crossed The Long Trail at the summit of Middlebury Gap yesterday and we crossed the Appalachian Trail at the unnamed summit just before dropping down to Woodstock today. A rain storm caught us at Middlebury Gap and it looked like one was waiting for us at the unnamed summit but we squeaked through and made it to town dry (the rain started just as we checked in to our motel).

I noticed the bike was steering a little "mushy" as we came down a long hill into East Thetford, VT this afternoon. Sure enough, it was a flat on the back. I was hoping we'd make it all the way to Bar Harbor on the current set of tires but, since we carry a spare, I went ahead and put on the new tire as the more rubber they have on them the less likely they are to be punctured. Hopefully, that flat will be our last. I would say I've fixed about ten flats on the trip so far.

We had a close call on the road this afternoon. A tractor from a roadside dairy pulling a huge tank filled with a pungent, soupy mixture of cow dung and urine pulled out onto the road in front of us. It lurched from a stop and because the farmer had forgotten to put the lid on the tank, a twenty-gallon swoosh of the vile liquid slopped out the top and splattered on the road in front of us sending Mary into hysterics. She was shrieking at me to slow down and I was laughing uncontrollably at the grossness of it all. When the tractor and its foul cargo were a hundred yards down the road several pickups roared by us too close, as they often do, and were soon right behind the tractor and crowding him. I was saying a little prayer that the tractor could lurch again at just the right moment and send another swoosh across their windshields but no such luck.

Some time ago it was decided that Mary needed more responsibilities and she was named official map reader. This is a big responsibility as we jump from one back road to another about twenty or more times a day. We used to have to stop and have me pull the map out of my bag each time we came to a junction. Now that Mary's doing the duty we can consult the map as we ride since she doesn't have to use her hands to steer the bike. If this happens while we're riding through town, passersby sometimes smile at the sight of the woman reading (complete with reading glasses) while she rides. I tell her to take it one step farther by attaching a book stand to her handlebars and reading a novel as we pedal along. (She's not interested.) I'm waiting for the electronic navigation system that will fasten to the handlebars and track the cyclist's progress on the maps against his true position with GPS. That way, we could actually see ourselves moving along the map and would know immediately if we took the wrong turn. How cool would that be? It's coming. Probably in a few years.

I have often written of my frustrations with my computer and web mail on this trip. I've managed to solve most of the problems with help from various sources but still have trouble emailing photos. And then…….I got to talking to the guy down the row in our motel and learned he used to be a computer engineer for Microsoft in Redmond, Washington. "Gee, what a coincidence!" I told him – "my computer uses Microsoft software" (as do about 95% of all personal computers). He is an immigrant from India who now works on Wall Street. He's traveling through New Hampshire to see the autumn leaves with his father who apparently doesn't speak English. Unfortunately, he was not able to resolve my problem because there is no Internet reception at this hotel. A golden opportunity lost if ever there was one.

Like a couple of high school seniors in May, we are nearing the end of our big adventure. It looks like we will arrive in Bar Harbor about October 8, four days from now and just in time to celebrate our 25th anniversary on October 10 which was our plan. We feel a great sense of accomplishment that we have been able to consistently make our miles for the last six weeks and see so much of our country close-up. Mary says she's had an incredible time on the trip but that she's ready for the trip to end. I'm not so sure I am. As I was riding today I was looking around at the hills and taking stock of my feelings. I'm still into the whole experience of finding out what is over the next mountain each day, of feeling that great feeling when the bike is moving easily along a country lane, of how *good* a drink from my water bottle tastes after riding up a long steep hill. Yeah, I like this way of life. I know it has to end though. I'm preparing myself for it.

October 5, 2006; Day 48; Mile 3808; Woodstock, NH to Norway, Maine: We left Woodstock under a watercolor sky and a brisk wind blowing. It was quite a change after the tropical air that has kept us "humidified" for several days.

This photo looks better in color. (See Mary?)
Woodstock and Lincoln, conjoined towns at the edge of the White Mountains, are thriving resort towns and no wonder: National Forest, ski resorts, and easily the most spectacular fall foliage we've seen on this trip.

Right at the edge of town the climb up to the 2855-ft. Kancamagus Summit (the highest since we crossed the Rockies) began but we were ready for it. We'd eaten a big breakfast, the air temperature was cool, and our bicycling muscles are as developed as they're gonna get. The climb went off without a hitch – we didn't even stop once. These mountains may not be as tall as the western ones but the roads up their flanks are steeper. This one had a relatively constant grade (a good thing) whereas several of the recent ones had excruciatingly steep sections interspersed with flat sections as if the highway engineers used old Indian trails as their guide.

The descent to Conway was steep, long, and cold despite the arrival of the long-absent sun. We had to sit on a sunny park bench and sip hot coffees for close to an hour before we had thawed enough to get back on the bike.

Mary warms herself with hot coffee and sunshine in Conway, NH park.

To give you some idea of the scale of things back east consider that it took us ten days to cross Montana and less than one each for Vermont and New Hampshire. So far, Maine is most noteworthy for the poor quality of its asphalt. We hit a bump on a steep downhill this afternoon and were lucky not to bend our wheel rims. Some of the grades on these little back roads have to be close to 20%!

Bought some Gold Bond foot powder for my shoes which have redefined the concept of foot odor. I hadn't worn them before this trip and found out too late that they're a little too small so I've had to wear them without socks to make them fit. As a result I've learned that socks serve another purpose besides keeping your feet warm – they sop up foot sweat and make it hard for odor-causing bacteria to set up camp in your shoes. My shoes are obviously now hosting the Genghis Kahn of bacteria and his entire Mongol horde.

Since we're only days from the trip's end I thought it about time to make some arrangements for getting home which I did on-line with Amtrak. We're riding the train home from Portland, Maine to Wenatchee – leaving the 11th and arriving the 14th. We'll have a couple of days in Bar Harbor to see the sights which I have heard are spectacular. We'll probably have to pack the bike in a big box and ship it as freight and then ride a bus down to Portland.

That mystery squeak our bike makes has become embarrassing it is so loud. When we pedal through populated areas we ease off a little because it sounds like we're riding an old clunker. At one point this afternoon, I was worried something essential was going to fall off and leave us stranded in rural Maine. While that would be a serious logistical problem it would almost be worth it to solve the mystery of what is making that sound. It drives me crazy! Every time we think we have noticed a pattern that may help pinpoint the source we test it and find out we were wrong. The sound has changed over time. It started out as a raspy noise and has progressed through what I would call a groan, moan, and squeak. Today a bird far off in the woods answered it with a similar cry. He or she apparently thought it was a mating call. That's all we need – to be followed by a lovesick bird attempting to woo our bicycle. At times it sounds exactly like something is happening on an old spring mattress upstairs. Today it also sounded like a crosscut saw cutting through a 2X4. What is that sound? I have to know.

October 6, 2006; Day 49; Mile 3888; Norway to Newcastle, Maine: We have reached the Atlantic! Newcastle is a harbor town of about 2000 on Maine's central coast with a 12-ft. tide that surges as a raging torrent under the bridge that connects it to nearby Damariscotta. Tides like this give engineers ideas about hydroelectric power generation although there is no evidence that anyone has harnessed that particular source here yet.

There was frost in Norway (Maine) this morning but a brilliant sun to take the sting out of our fingers during our first hour. All in all, it was a strange day of riding. From Norway to Newcastle the countryside is covered by pine trees with a dash of hardwoods thrown in for color. There are no mountains to speak of but the terrain certainly isn't flat. Rather, it undulates in every direction but never more than a few hundred feet. The perspective of a bicycle rider passing through it is what I imagine a sailor lost at sea would see with his head just above water in twenty-foot swells. Only when at the crest of a hill (wave) can you see anything but the trees (sea) immediately around you. The road is winding in the extreme and the total effect is quite disorienting. If the sun hadn't been in plain view by which to orient myself I would have had no idea if we were heading north or south.

Maine is a poor state in its interior. The roads are decrepit and the houses run down. From what I've heard, farming has never been profitable in Maine's thin, boggy soil but in these parts no one even attempts to work a farm any more. There is no apparent industry other than the occasional logging trucks which seem to specialize in menacing bicycle riders on the state's mostly shoulder-less roads. But it's beautiful country all the same. Flaming-red maple trees and lichen-covered stone walls abound. Mill ponds and villages with crooked streets speak of another century.

As I mentioned earlier, there were no mountains to climb today but that doesn't mean the riding was easy. By early afternoon Mary was grumbling and threatening to find an Interstate to ride on because of the constant up-and-down terrain. It was not unusual, especially as we neared Newcastle, to pass through the climb-and-descend cycle of one or two hundred feet five times in the length of one mile. Add up all the little climbs we did today and I wouldn't be surprised if it surpassed our day crossing the Rocky Mountains in Montana. One and a half days out of our final destination and we are actually thinking about leaving Adventure Cycling's prescribed route to look for better engineered roads. Mary is of the opinion that she has earned an easy ride into Bar Harbor.

Late in the day our discussion turned to our chances of getting a decent room for the evening. We realized that the chances weren't good because of the combination of it being: 1) Friday 2) Columbus Day weekend 3) autumn leaf season. We actually became quite glum at the prospect of arriving in Newcastle and having no place to stay. Our guide map only listed one B&B. With Mary's mental motel detection radar set on "HIGH SENSITIVITY" as we rode into town we were ready to settle for any roof over our heads at any price but elated to notice a "Vacancy" sign in front of a nice looking inn. So afraid were we that another tourist would beat us to this lucky bit of good fortune that I had to make a conscious effort not to run breathlessly into the inn and slap a wad of cash on the counter to claim "first dibs" on the room. And good fortune it turned out to be – our room has superb furnishings – even a fireplace which we are putting to good use on this chilly evening by the sea. Our hostess is a gracious Katherine Hepburnesque woman with a faint Maine accent. The room is every bit as nice as the posh room we splurged on at Niagara Falls. In fact, the whole inn looks like a photo spread in one of those home decorating magazines. I make no claim to possessing "good taste" or even knowing what it is but I look around this room and everything looks *right*.

October 7, 2006; Day 50; Mile 3965; Newcastle to East Orland, Maine: Got off to a late start this morning (9:30 AM) but I'm not complaining. Breakfast was quite an experience at the Harbor View Inn. We sat down to our assigned seats (our names were printed on the menus) and ate several courses served on fine china with the food arranged perfectly and decorated with tiny flowers and herbs. It was good food but the portions were selected more with dieting women in mind than bicycling men. Knowing that a hard day of pedaling lay ahead, I hurried to our room after breakfast and supplemented the tiny muffin and baked pear with a king size Snickers bar.

The food portions may have been small but the conversation was lively as we traded stories with a couple from Cleveland over breakfast. They seemed fascinated by our journey across the country. Mary was into the whole fancy-dancy experience like a little girl dressed up for a tea party with her friends (was that her little finger pointing toward the ceiling as she held her coffee cup to her mouth?)

Also at the breakfast table was an old guy with a long gray beard who was another guest at the inn. He didn't say much until breakfast was almost over and then he abruptly announced that he stripped the insulation off copper wire and then sold the copper as scrap metal for a living. He went on to explain that he did this with the aid of a razor knife and that he obtained about three pounds of copper on a typical day. Knowing that copper is not gold I dared not ask him the relevant question at that point – how much did he get per pound for the copper? The woman from

Cleveland failed to see where that question would lead and popped the question for me. When the old guy answered that the price of copper was high right now at two dollars per pound she paused for a second to do a little quick mental multiplication and then stared at me in disbelief. Since the old guy's room cost about $180 I restrained myself from observing "Let's see, Old Man, that means you worked thirty days to earn the money for your room last night." No one at the table wanted to touch subject after that and the old man resumed his silent presence at the end of the table. The paradox of how he afforded the room was later answered when he told us his son had paid for the room.

The day was quintessentially autumnal with a bright blue sky, cool temperatures and abundant sun. We stayed close to the ocean on US 1 most of the day with the rocky seashore on our starboard and historic homes, colorful trees and stone walls on our port. The twin towns of Rockport and Camden were sufficiently "New Englandy" with their Colonial architecture, granite street curbs, and harbors filled with sail boats, to be crammed with tourists come to Maine to see the autumn leaves. Locals call them "leaf peepers." There must have been a hundred bed & breakfasts on US 1 north of Camden. We're more kindly disposed toward the institution after our stay at the Harbor View.

Mortar-less stone walls (what I build for a living in Wenatchee) are everywhere to be seen along this section of the Maine coast. Unlike the impoverished interior of the state, well-appointed homes line the coastline and stone walls are *de rigueur* in these neighborhoods. Along one short stretch of the highway near Lincolnville there are three commercial landscaping firms which specialize in stone work.

A magnificent new suspension bridge is being constructed across the Penobscot River between Verona and Bucksport to replace the narrow, rusted relic we crossed today. Talk about bicycle unfriendly! The old bridge's deck is steel grate and its sidewalks are about 18" wide. We had to walk on the narrow, plywood sidewalk and push our bike on the bridge deck with the traffic. A sign near the entrance of the new bridge says it will open for business in fall of 2006 which is about *now* on my calendar. Judging by the way the job is going I'd say they'll be lucky to open by next summer.

We overtook a middle-aged couple touring on a tandem bike near Searsport. They are the only tandem bikers we have met on the entire trip. They are from Dallas, Texas and were heading to Bar Harbor too but had only ridden their bike from Portland, Maine. We easily trumped their ride with our cross-country credentials which they promptly trumped by announcing that they had sailed around the world in their sail boat. They had also biked elsewhere extensively, including a 1500-mile trip in Australia so we had a short, intense, and noisy conversation on the roadside as the constant traffic streamed by.

Mary wasn't feeling well when we arrived at our motel. She has been puking for the last hour. She suspects an egg salad sandwich she had for lunch.

p.s. Mary is now asleep beside me so she must be feeling better.

October 8, 2006; Day 51; Mile 4000; East Orland to Bar Harbor, Maine: Bar Harbor! BAR HARBOR! **BAR HARBOR!** Or, as the locals say Bah Hahbah – they really do. Like the heading says, 51 days and 4000 miles exactly and we are finally here. But first, I have another tale to tell……

Journey's end in Bar Harbor, Maine.

It begins (we think) at a convenience store on US 1 in Stockton Springs at which we had stopped yesterday afternoon to refuel ourselves for the final push to Bucksport, the day's destination – I on two slices of pepperoni pizza and Mary on an egg salad sandwich. Bucksport's motels were full of leaf peepers so we rode another seven miles to East Orland where we rented a no-frills little cabin at the Pine Shore Motel. On the way there Mary mentioned, off-hand, that she was experiencing a little "gut rumble." An hour later at dinner she stopped halfway through her plate of spaghetti saying it was good spaghetti but she just didn't feel like eating anymore.

When we got back to our cabin she began contorting herself in various yoga-like positions saying she had gas and needed to get it out. In another hour she said the intestinal pain was very uncomfortable and asked me to ask the hotel owner if she had any medicine for gas (the Pine Shore Motel is not near any store where one could buy medicine.) The owner searched her medicine cabinet and came back with some Tums antacid tablets saying those were all she had. Mary swallowed a couple of them but they didn't help.

I was coming out of the bathroom, having just plugged in my computer there to the wall outlet for recharging (at the only 3-pronged electrical socket in the cabin) when Mary sprang from the bed with a look of alarm in her eyes and ran past me into the bathroom where she immediately began vomiting into the toilet. The vomiting seemed to give her some relief and Mary went back to bed and fell asleep.

At one o'clock in the morning Mary woke me up and said she felt much worse. She said her intestinal pain was unbearable and said she needed medical help. But without a car and in a little isolated motel in the middle of the night, where does one get medical help? The motel office was locked up and darkened but she insisted I rouse the owner and get an ambulance if need be. I knocked on the door, politely at first, then louder and louder. No answer. I returned to our cabin and told Mary. She was writhing in bed and insisted I get help no matter what I had to do. I returned and started pounding on the owner's windows. She eventually came to the door. I told her the situation was dire and asked where the nearest hospital was. She told me it was twelve miles up the road in Ellsworth and handed me the keys to her car.

Ellsworth's hospital is little but it has a 24-hour emergency room and we were very happy to walk – I in the usual way, Mary bent over in pain – through the doors into the waiting arms of their concerned staff. "Severe abdominal pain" my RN wife said immediately. They got her on a stretcher, drew some blood for tests, and hooked her up to an I-V immediately. A shot of morphine and some anti-nausea medicine were soon administered and Mary settled down. The doctor looked over the test results and said it looked like food poisoning to her. The prime suspect? – that egg salad sandwich. Since there is no treatment other than symptom relief they pumped Mary full of saline and sent us on our way.

When we got back to our cabin it was nearly dawn. Mary plopped into bed and fell asleep. I got a little sleep too but soon found myself lying in bed considering our situation and wondering how it would turn out. I didn't know how Mary's recovery would go. The doctor at the hospital seemed to think it would be several days before she would feel well enough to ride the bicycle. If so, that would throw off our carefully planned schedule. There we were, just 40 miles from our destination and stranded in a little cabin on the highway. At the very least, I figured, I was looking at a long, boring day while Mary recuperated.

About 10AM Mary woke up, looked around our room and announced "We gotta' get out of this place." She didn't know if she would have the strength to pedal to Bar Harbor but I was so overjoyed at the prospect of getting there that I told her "If I have to, I'll tie you on the bike seat and pedal you to Bar Harbor." We loaded up, profusely thanked the motel owner for her help and pedaled off.

To my immense relief and her credit, Mary was soon supplying her usual share of our propulsion. The morning sun was surprisingly warm. A sea breeze added the perfect touch for our final leg of the journey. Just outside of Bar Harbor a couple in a Subaru pulled up beside us at a stop light and asked where we had come from. When the Subaru's female passenger learned we had come clear across the country, she got so into talking to us that she would have talked right through the green traffic light if I had not started pedaling. They pulled off the road a few blocks ahead and waved us over. They also owned a tandem bike, they said, and peppered us with questions. They were thinking of doing a cross-country ride. The subject so excited her she was literally jumping up and down. They invited us to stay at their house in Bar Harbor which we would be passing on our way into town. Sure enough, when we passed it, they had placards along the road with the messages "CONGRATULATIONS TEAM TANDEM FROM WASHINGTON!!" and the like. Mary said she thought they would actually do the ride. I had to agree. It felt good to think that what we have done may inspire other people. It's not every day that you get to inspire someone.

October 10, 2006; Portland, Maine: After our triumphant entry into Bar Harbor on October 8 we spent a quiet day coming down from our end-of-trip high. Much of yesterday was used to accomplish such mundane tasks as laundry, arranging for a local bike store to pack up our bike and ship it back to Washington, and arranging transportation for us to Portland. Mary was still feeling the aftereffects of her food poisoning in the form of wrenched abdominal muscles and wanted to rest so I spent the afternoon hiking to the top of the mountain behind town. Someone had built a stone staircase of local granite to the top (2 miles!) The view from the mountaintop was so spectacular – the autumn leaves, islands, ocean, and the visiting ocean liner, Queen Mary II, in the harbor – that I lingered for over an hour exulting in the serenity of it all.

Our original plan was to be in Bar Harbor for our 25th anniversary which is today but instead we find ourselves in the less than romantic city of Portland because lack of foresight forced us to be here to catch the Amtrak at 6:20 tomorrow morning. We rode a bus into town, our trusty bicycle now in the care of the United Parcel Service and no longer available for the riding. We are looking forward to relaxing on the train, reading, and contemplating where we've been and what we've done for the last fifty days. We're hoping we get to see much of the same territory we pedaled through from the glass-enclosed vista car atop the train.

Our anniversary celebration is pretty low-key which is understandable with Mary still feeling kind of sick. No champagne toasts or romantic dinners this evening. I walked over to a nearby mall and bought myself a new pair of running shoes to replace my stinky ones while Mary slept. Like I said – pretty low-key for an anniversary celebration. Even so, I wonder if our moods aren't a little more subdued than even Mary's illness can explain. I suspect there is a little of the let-down blues happening here, exacerbated by Mary's illness. You come to the end of your journey which has been your goal for so long and you have put so much effort into getting here and you build your arrival up to something spectacular and necessarily somewhat unrealistic and of course it's going to let you down. You set yourself up for it. I think this is more the case for Mary than for me. I wish she were feeling better because I'd do my best to take her out on the town and try to make this evening special.

I think this end-of-journey blues is common. I remember years ago reading an article in *National Geographic* about two guys who crossed the Northwest Passage in small boats and when they reached the end of their journey one of them descended into a profound funk just when you would think it would be time to celebrate. Not that I'm in a funk but I do have some inkling what the guy was talking about. For me, it's that you have been living this charmed existence because you have absolute fixation on life's goal during the journey and you've been encountering new things everyday and suddenly it all ends and you don't know quite what to make of it.

As for the 25th anniversary part of this trip, I suppose I should have something meaningful to say now. I've been waiting for the words of wisdom to channel through me into this keypad but so far not much has arrived. I think it's because Mary and I have been so close, literally - physically, for this trip that there hasn't been the time for any perspective about our relationship. She and I have not been out of each other's sight in almost two months and when somebody is right there beside you, you don't have to think about them in the abstract because you have an actual physical body to deal with.

Of course, there is the obvious metaphor of a journey across the country and marriage being a journey through life. In our case, both have worked, probably for the same reasons although neither of us is very clear as to what the particular reasons are. For my part, the best I can come up with is to say it all comes back to *liking* Mary. That may sound like nothing more than a watered down version of *loving* Mary but it's not. What I mean to say is that there has never been a time when I have not wanted to be around her. I enjoy her company and that means a lot coming from a basically anti-social person like me. I can't think of anyone else I could say that about. It's not because she is extraordinary in any of the usual variety of human attributes – clever, funny, etc. But I know enough about how I respond to people to know that none of those things would matter much to me if she weren't genuine. Perhaps that is it – she has never tried to put anything over on me, to be someone she isn't, to impress me through deception. I don't think she puts forth much effort to be genuine – it comes naturally to her but it captivates me.

We have been through a lot together, obviously, after 25 years and this journey can only add to our reservoir of shared experience – a bank upon which we can draw in rough times. When you've pedaled, just the two of you, over Montana's mountains and through the drenching rain in Sodus Point, you have a special bond. When you've got a quality dame like Mary for a wife you've got something special. I'm a lucky man and this trip and my wife are proof of that.

Appendices

The Pioneer

As far as I've been able to determine, there is no official estimate of how many people ride bicycles across the United States each year. There certainly is no national register or, if there is, we never heard of it and didn't sign it. More often than not, I suspect, riders are simply people who decide they want to go "a-wanderin'" and do just that with a minimum of fanfare. No one keeps track of their accomplishment. My guess is that the yearly number is in the thousands, maybe a few tens of thousands which would make such a ride an achievement less common than running a marathon but significantly more common than, say, climbing Mt. Everest.

That appraisal of difficulty is based on modern bicycle technology and the plethora of lightweight clothing and gear available today. Crossing the country on a bicycle in 1884, however, was a proposition of an altogether different order of magnitude when a young Englishman named Thomas Stevens became the first person to do so. A onetime miner of modest means,

Stevens was an avid consumer of the plentiful travel literature of his time and determined to make his mark in the annals of adventure. Shortly after purchasing a 50-inch penny-farthing bicycle, Stevens set off from San Francisco bound for Boston on April 22, 1884. His penny-farthing (so named because its two wheels' relative sizes were roughly in the same ratio as the English coins of the same names) represented the most advanced cycle technology of the time. On those rare occasions when a suitably long stretch of smooth riding surface was available, it could be pedaled at speeds up to the then-phenomenal velocity of twenty miles per hour. The penny-farthing's technology was basically that of a two-wheeled tricycle in that the pedals were attached directly to the axle of the large front wheel. The large diameter of the front wheel was necessary to magnify the pedal stroke sufficiently to reach high speed in the absence of a lightweight chain and gear assembly which was beyond the technology of the day. The front wheel's diameter was largely determined by the rider's inseam – tall men rode tall penny-farthings. Having the rider positioned high above the wheel's axle made penny-farthing riders whose front wheel's progress was impeded by a pothole or stone in the road susceptible to "taking a header" – a dangerous and undignified maneuver in which the rider found himself ejected over the handlebars like a stone from a slingshot.

The transcontinental railroad had been completed in 1869, a mere fifteen years before Thomas set off from San Francisco and paved roads in the interior of the country were non-existent in 1884 so Thomas, of necessity, often found himself walking his bicycle through long stretches of sandy soil or wet, sticky clay. Railroad beds of wooden ties were too bumpy to ride on but in many areas were the only passable surface. Since he crossed the Sierra Nevada in spring when snow was still ten feet deep he stuck exclusively to the railroad while traversing those mountains. In many places the tracks were covered by extensive snow sheds that extended ten or more miles at a stretch. Encountering a coal-burning, steam locomotive in one of those snow sheds was literally a life-and-death experience where he found himself clinging to the wall of the shed while the passing train came within inches of dragging his trembling body to a bloody death. Ironically, he reported that he made his best progress in several remote areas of the West where he encountered dry lake beds on which he was able to realize his bicycle's high-speed potential.

To my mind, the most amazing aspect of Stevens' journey was his lack of provisions. He rarely carried any food and the sum total of his gear was a small handlebar bag that contained a pair of socks, a shirt, a raincoat and a Smith & Wesson .38 revolver. His *modus operandi* was to depend on the kindness of strangers and to a large extent it served him well. Time and again he would ride up to the front door of an isolated cabin in the vast expanse of the continent's interior and present himself as a wayfarer in need of food and lodging whereupon the startled homeowner would oblige him with whatever meager hospitality he or she could manage. Occasionally, circumstances were such that he spent a cold and miserable night sleeping in the open with nothing more substantial than his raincoat for warmth and shelter. More often, his strategy when there was no shelter to be found was to ride through the night to stay warm. On one such midnight ride through northern Nevada he found his way illuminated by a large moon that inspired him to write:

"....a more beautiful sight than the one that now greets [me] is scarcely possible to conceive. Only those who have been in this inter-mountain country can have any idea of a glorious moonlit night in the clear atmosphere of this dry, elevated region. It is almost as light as day, and one can see to ride quite well wherever the road is ridable. The pale moon seems to fill the whole broad valley with a flood of soft, silvery light; the peaks of many snowy mountains loom up white and spectral; the stilly air broken by the excited yelping of a pack of coyotes noisily baying the pale-yellow author of all this loveliness......"

The sight of a man on a bicycle on the lonely prairie of Wyoming or Nebraska in 1884 was indeed something to behold. Many of the people he encountered didn't even know that such a thing as a bicycle existed and the vast majority of them had never seen one. He often found himself demonstrating to disbelieving audiences that it was *possible* to ride a two-wheeled vehicle. Those who hadn't witnessed his arrival atop the penny-farthing couldn't imagine how such a vehicle could balance without a third and fourth wheel. One evening in Carlin, Nevada, there being no suitable place to ride out-of-doors, he found himself proving to a group of skeptical cowboys that the penny-farthing was ridable by riding in circles around the tavern's interior. A collision with a low-hanging chandelier on that occasion nearly cost him his scalp.

Another incident that puts Stevens' journey in historical perspective is his oft-cited encounter with "prairie schooners," or covered wagons heading west. Even though by 1884 the transcontinental railroad was the preferred mode of transportation for most people who traveled west, some poor families from Arkansas and Missouri were still making the trip with all their possessions in canvas-covered, ox-drawn wagons.

Stevens often showed himself to be an acute observer of social trends who didn't shy away from passing judgment on those he met. He noted that the Digger Indians of the western foothills of the Sierras lived in "chronic wretchedness" and that their energy had been "well-nigh eradicated" while the Washoe Indians near the summit of the Sierras were a lively and curious bunch. He was disdainful of many of the inhabitants of Nevada and Utah whose livelihoods had been undermined by the coming of the railroad and who refused to adapt, preferring to mourn their loss and find comfort in alcohol and bitterness. On the other hand, he was much impressed by the industry of Utah's Mormons and the communistic Germans of Iowa's Amana Society.

He was very much a man of his times when it came to how he employed his revolver when he encountered wildlife. He kept a "game-list" which was a kind of scorecard similar to that used by modern-day birders on which he kept a running tally of all the animals he killed for no other reason than to add impressive length to his list. He often displayed a droll sense of humor when describing his encounters with the unfortunate animals that made his game-list as in this description of the demise of a rattlesnake that had sunk its fangs into his canvas gaiters:

"Giving his snakeship to understand that I don't appreciate his "good intentions" by vigorously shaking him off, I turned my "barker" loose on him, and quickly convert him into a "goody-good snake;" for if "the only good Indian is a dead one," surely the same terse remark applies with much greater force to the vicious and deadly rattler."

Because his route closely shadowed the railroad, eastbound trains often spread word of his coming to towns along the way in advance of his arrival. In Laramie, Wyoming, a small group of forward-thinking young men had formed a bicycle club and rode out to greet him. Wherever he encountered fellow bicyclists along the way he was hailed as a hero and given the warm welcome he so richly deserved.

His entire, 3500-mile trip across the United States took him 103 days of which 83 were spent traveling and twenty as layovers due to inclement weather. That works out to an average of 42 miles per travel day which borders on the astounding when one considers the conditions of his ride. Roads were little more than wagon-wheel ruts for much of the journey. His penny-farthing was, in effect, a bicycle that was always in high gear so hill climbs were either unbelievably difficult or impossible. The surfaces he traveled on were such that he estimates he actually walked a good portion of the total distance because riding simply wasn't possible.

He spent the winter following his ride in New York where his exploits were publicized in the magazine *Outsider*. The following spring he boarded a steamer for Liverpool, England and proceeded, over the next two years, to bicycle through Europe and Asia to complete the first 'round-the-world journey. Those exploits he published in various magazines and later, collectively, as a book called *Around the World on a Bicycle*.

Race Across America

The number of miles covered each day is a number that loomed large in our thoughts on this trip. We had figured that we needed to average a minimum of 70 miles per day to complete the 4000 miles to Bar Harbor by October 10. That meant we had to do in excess of 70 miles whenever possible to give ourselves a comfortable cushion because any delays due to illness, accidents, mechanical problems, or rest days would put us behind schedule and have to be made up by some hard riding. Because we had ridden 100 miles per day on a four-day bicycle ride the previous year, we figured we would be able to cover that many miles on this trip once we worked out the bugs of the first week.

As it turned out, we did in excess of 100 miles on several days. The most we ever did was 135 miles in a single day. But riding through the flat corn fields of Illinois with a tail wind can hardly be compared to riding up hill against a headwind in North Dakota so mileage was bound to fluctuate wildly. The most meaningful measure of the rate at which a rider is progressing across the country is the average number of miles covered for the entire trip and for us that number turned out to be very close to 80.

People who have never ridden a bicycle any significant distance might wonder what a reasonable number of miles to ride in a day is. To someone who hasn't ridden a bicycle in years, twenty miles would probably result in considerable muscle soreness and fatigue. When I was about thirteen and a Boy Scout I remember reading the requirements for earning a bicycling merit badge. As I recall they had the would-be bicyclist start with several modest rides of ten miles, work up to several twenties and the grand finale was a fifty-miler. That seemed intimidatingly long to me then – so much so that I never did earn that merit badge.

Most of the riders we encountered on our trip told us they were averaging anywhere from 40 to 100 miles per day. I would say the overall average for all the riders was in the 60- to 70-mile range. John, probably the strongest rider we met, told us he was averaging 99 miles per day. Mind you, all of these people were carrying significant extra weight in the form of panniers or trailers full of gear which slows a rider down considerably.

To me, this train of thought begs the question "How fast could someone cross the United States on a bicycle if he were in peak physical condition and he rode as hard and as long as he could?" You might be surprised to learn (I was) that this question is answered anew each year when a small number of dedicated ultra-marathon cyclists race each other in the not-too-well-known competition called Race Across America, or RAAM. I vaguely remembered watching such a race on television in the early 1980's but thought it had been a one-time event. I did a little research on the Internet and was surprised to learn that RAAM has been held every year since 1982 up to the present.

RAAM is different from its more famous cousins like the Tour de France and Tour d'Italia which are so-called stage races. In a stage race, the course is broken down into a series of fixed-length, one-day rides or stages, usually about 100 to 150 miles in length. At the completion of each stage, the riders are able to rest and recuperate until the next day's stage. The stage race format is generally preferred in the bicycle racing world because the riders start together at the beginning of each stage and are therefore more likely to be "neck-and-neck" at the finish which is the way most spectators like it. Stage racing also allows riders to "draft" behind other riders which significantly reduces the amount of effort required to maintain a particular pace and therefore leads to the *peleton* or pack riding which introduces a whole different strategy than would otherwise be the case.

RAAM on the other hand, is run as if it were one, giant, 3000-mile stage. From the time riders leave the west coast until they arrive on the east coast there are no scheduled breaks. If a rider were capable of riding non-stop across the country, RAAM rules allow, indeed, encourage this. As far as RAAM riders are concerned, sleep is a wasteful activity that eats up valuable road time. Riding several days without sleep is not uncommon. Indeed, being able to tolerate lengthy periods of sleep deprivation is a mandatory quality for a competitive RAAM racer, some of whom average as little as ninety minutes of sleep per day during the race. As you might guess, sleep deprivation takes a certain toll on the human brain and it is not at all uncommon for racers to hallucinate in the latter stages of the race. Hallucinating riders have been observed to turn around and ride in the wrong direction, convinced they are right despite protests from their support crew. They get off their bikes and start feeling the asphalt to see if it's "real," report aliens are looking at them from bushes along the road, see lengthy series of hieroglyphic messages in the cracks in the road and suspect their own support crew members of plotting against them. Michael Shermer, a veteran RAAM racer and psychologist who has first-hand experience with sleep-deprived hallucination, is convinced that such hallucination is actually a condition where the brain begins to dream while the rider is still awake.

Whereas Tour d' France riders put in 100 to 150 miles during a typical day, the best RAAM riders sometimes exceed 400 miles a day. Stage racing is usually a crowded affair with large "clumps" of riders and often large numbers of spectators. RAAM is often a solitary journey little appreciated by anyone but the racers and a small number of dedicated admirers. Because the course is the entire width of the United States, racers are often hundreds of miles apart. It is not uncommon for RAAM racers to never see one of their competitors after the first few days of the race.

So what inspires RAAM racers to endure the physical and mental hardships of this race? Certainly not the fame and riches that often are the rewards of top-notch athletes. Prize money amounts at most to a few thousand dollars that doesn't even cover the expenses incurred by the racers. For those who complete the race within 48 hours of the winner there is a gold RAAM ring. For many entrants, there is no tangible reward – only the satisfaction of knowing they have tested themselves against one of the most rigorous standards ever devised. When the race was televised via ABC's Wide World of Sports from 1982 to 1986, a modicum of fame may have inspired entrants but no longer. RAAM hasn't been televised since 1986 and it receives scant publicity in the popular press. Clearly, the usual motivators at work in world-class athletics are absent in RAAM. Perhaps Lon Haldeman, winner of the first two RAAMs and a legend among RAAM riders, expressed the true motivation best when he said "You couldn't pay me enough to ride this race." Motivation to compete in RAAM in most cases seems to be an intensely personal challenge that the racers set for themselves. They want to prove to themselves and a small number of friends and family that they have the inordinate ration of grit that this ultimate test of endurance requires.

Fewer than half of the people who have started RAAM races over the years have gone the full distance to the east coast. You might suspect this high rate of casualty is due to poorly-prepared, dilettante entries but nothing could be further from the truth. Qualifying for a RAAM is a major athletic achievement in its own right. Only a tiny fraction of those who enter RAAM qualifying races each year are invited to enter the big race itself.

Any number of problems can ruin the hopes of RAAM riders. Many of them succumb to the enormous physical strain of continually pushing their bodies day after day and through the night. Knees that give out are a common story. Neck muscles that fail altogether have ended the ambitions of more than a few riders. Neck muscle problems manifest themselves when the riders find they simply can no longer hold their heads erect enough to see the road ahead. Ingenious support crews have been known to support their racer's drooping head from fishing-pole-like cantilevers or through the use of counterweights to do what necks no longer can.

Perhaps no part of the body of a long-distance bicycle rider is more susceptible to catastrophic failure than the regions of the body in contact with the bicycle seat. "Acres of blisters" is how one rider described his backside after crossing the finish line. Excruciating, bleeding sores are a common malady. One female rider literally cast modesty to the wind when she cut away large patches of her bicycle shorts in the hope that increased airflow would relieve the "fire down there."

All of these physical ailments often contribute to profound despair as well. No one gets through RAAM without a great deal of suffering. For many riders, the physical pain, sleep deprivation, and the disappointment of finding themselves far behind where they hoped they would be after several days of continual racing are too overwhelming to contemplate any more. They get off their bikes and go home; abandoning a dream they have already sacrificed years of their lives to.

Outside magazine once conducted a poll of sports writers as to what is the most demanding athletic feat. The writers compared such events as the Olympic marathon, the Tour de France, swimming the English Channel, climbing Mt. Everest, etc. RAAM was chosen as the most demanding race of all.

In the cycling world, the Tour de France by far receives the most attention. In the years after its inauguration, RAAM devotees touted their race as the ultimate test of endurance, i.e. harder than the Tour. Tour devotees either dismissed or ignored their claims. The question was put to the test in 1985 when three-time Tour de France cyclist Jonathan Boyer signed up for RAAM. Among American bike racers, Boyer was rated second only to Tour winner Greg LeMond. Boyer won RAAM that year but only by four hours over the second-place finisher. Four hours at the finish line of RAAM is considered a photo-flash finish. Not only was the 1985 race close but the 1986 winner, Pete Penseyres, bested Boyer's time by seventeen hours. By showing that RAAM riders could give a Tour rider a run for his money, RAAM devotees felt vindicated. RAAM had been shown to be a world-class event.

So how fast can a man on a bicycle cross the United States? In the 1992 RAAM, American Rob Kish did it in 8 days, 3 hours, and 11 minutes – on a bicycle! Think about it. The first time I drove across the country it took me longer than that – in a car!